MOMMY, WHERE DO CUSTOMERS COME FROM?

HOW TO MARKET TO

A NEW WORLD OF

CONNECTED CUSTOMERS

By Larry Bailin

Foreword by Harry Beckwtih,
International best selling author of
"Selling the Invisible"

ACKNOWLEDGEMENTS

There are a few people I would like to thank that have helped me along the way and continue to support and encourage my antics. These are not in any particular order so those of you at the bottom of the list are just as important as those at the top, so get over it. At least I put you in here. What other books are you in?

My parents. If it were not for you both I would not be where I am today – literally. Thanks for the never-ending support and encouragement.

The incredibly talented people I work with, whose behavior and strange idiosyncrasies provide me a constant source of entertainment. You are all amazing and, for all you do, I thank you from the bottom of my heart. A special thanks to Elayne, Jim, Caryl, Jeff, Dan, Cathy, Vicky, Dave, Alex, Marilyn, John and the Coach.

My friends. I'm fortunate to have some of the finest friends for whom anyone could ask. You've been there through the best and worst of times, and I often wonder when the hell you're going to leave! You're just like family to me, and you all know how I treat my family. Thanks for everything.

My family. Thanks for all the support over the years. Putting up with me during my annoying years (that includes the last 20 years, plus this one and the next 15).

Last but certainly not least, Nicole. You are there through it all. You live with me and put up with me and that alone is no easy feat. You encourage me and bring light into my life and make me strive to be better – I love you.

Oh, I almost forgot! Thank you – the reader – for purchasing this book. I hope you find the information you are about to read informative, helpful and money well spent – no refunds!

INTRODUCTION I

With the growth and development of the Internet, the great technological flood continues to forever alter our communication abilities and methods. New and developing medium such as Internet search engines, email, blog's, podcasts, WiFi, Bluetooth, and PDA/Smart Phones are already impacting our global ability to communicate, collaborate, and market.

For the last twelve years, companies from virtually every conceivable stratum have been struggling to understand the Internet's impact on traditional business methods. Since the first days of the "Commercial Internet", and through the highs and lows of the "Dot Com" craze, the world has watched both Fortune 500 and local micro businesses make attempts to reap the rewards of success in this new world.

This book explains the changes one can make to successfully market and sell products and services to the critical new breed of techno-savvy customers. Based on market trends and new communication advancements, this customer represents the present and future for your business – and for every business.

What do these "connected customers" want? How are they different from customers of the past? What changes do you need to make to your business and in the way you communicate?

The answer to each of these questions will be provided within the confines of this book, as will a resolution to the burning question…

Mommy, where do customers come from?

As a tried and true, "Jersey Boy", this is where my rise to mediocrity started. Born and raised in Essex County, New Jersey (this explains my attitude), I lived in the Newark area (this explains my paranoia) until my family moved to Irvington (this explains the scar on my right shoulder) in the late 1970's. I took up art at an early age, enrolling in advanced art classes throughout grammar school and high school. Upon graduation, I attended The Newark School of Art for further classical art training, and developed a genuine passion for commercial art and marketing. Choosing to follow this path, I continued my marketing education at a local community college, completing a fledgling computer graphics program, and obtaining an AA in Fine Art.

My formal education complete, I became a serial entrepreneur and my true education began. (My boundless wit blossomed, as well.) Having first identified sales as a necessary skill, I became quickly enamored of the process, and began to immerse myself in its various philosophies, while developing a technique of my own. I began reading sales and marketing-related books. (As far as I'm concerned, they are one and the same.) One after another, I devoured each of them like a child through a chocolate bar. Enthralled by authors such as Harry Beckwith, Zig Ziglar, Tom Hopkins, Seth Godin, and many others, I began to integrate all of their teachings into my own personal sales and marketing style.

Selling remains a crucial part of my life. I've never looked at sales as a "necessary evil" or dirty word. Selling is an art; a skill that allows me to help my clients make good decisions and grow their businesses. Selling helps me to deliver critical messages during vital moments.

I remain, to this day, a strict student of sales and continue to further my own education. Over the years, I've even had the distinct pleasure of meeting some of my teachers. I've shared the speakers' platform with Seth Godin, as well as dinner with Harry Beckwith and his lovely wife, Christine Clifford Beckwith, a true sales giant in her own right. In fact, even after having met sales superstars like Jeffrey Gitomer and Brian Tracy, you can still consistently find me perusing sales and marketing titles at the local Barnes & Noble. (I'm the one with the devil-may-care good looks, and grande cup of caffeine.)

Truth is, I've never been short on ideas. Back in the day, I launched some part-time businesses, trying things such as freelance art and neon sign design. Still, I never truly found my personal path toward success until around 1995.

I tend to think of 1995 as the true dawn of the "Commercial Internet." This is the year I co-founded Online Resources Incorporated (ORI). ORI designed, developed, marketed, and hosted websites and applications for the small to medium business market. Having started the company with four partners, we delivered over 200 customers within those first two years. This was a particularly amazing feat, considering that we didn't know what the hell we were doing, and fought constantly.

The fact remains that I knew nothing about the Internet when I started ORI. Still, being no stranger to Barnes & Noble, it wasn't long before I found myself being classified as an expert by people of influence within the industry. (I also found myself in the throes of a deepening coffee addiction.)

As was the norm back in those early "Dot Com" days, ORI was acquired by Planet Technology Solutions (PTS), a technology development company in Parsippany, NJ. After the acquisition, I remained at PTS as Director of e-Business, having been charged with expansion into new business areas for the rapidly growing company. In this capacity, I collaborated on high-level projects for major corporations such as Chanel, Hershey, Wrigley's, Dannon, Yankee Candle, Zany Brainy, and others.

In 1999, I pioneered an Internet Marketing Division for PTS. Heading up a team of technologists, marketers, managers and consultants, the division successfully created online marketing and search engine strategies for PTS clients. The Internet Marketing Division continued to grow over the next year and became an integral part of every e-Business strategy I developed.

All right, here we go again. In mid-2000, Vytek Wireless of White Plains, NY acquired Planet Technology Solutions. This was also about the time I began to get the entrepreneurial itch again. So, I took my leave of Vytek and the Hi-tech "Technology Solutions" industry, and founded Single Throw, my current company.

Life at Single Throw has been wonderful and our growing client list includes Scholastic, Hyperion Technologies, Select Energy, Oxford Health, Mag-Lite, Symbol Technologies, CentraState Healthcare, William Raveis Real Estate, BP Oil, Abel Energy, DeVry University, New Pig Corporation, Conair, Maglite, Harley-Davidson and many other public and private corporations.

Single Throw is an award winning Internet marketing company. We are currently at fifteen full-time employees and widely considered to be among the top Internet Marketers in the industry. In 2003, Single Throw was awarded a proclamation from the state of New Jersey for excellence in business and setting a standard in the Internet marketing industry. Also in 2003, Single Throw was nominated and accepted into the "Sherpa Marketing Guide" as one of the top companies in Internet marketing. In February of 2004, Single Throw appeared in best selling author Seth Godin's book "Bull Market", which is sponsored by Fast Company Magazine.

So…now it's official. I am considered an expert in the Internet marketing field and remain a sought after speaker on the topic of Internet marketing. I speak throughout the country on the topic of the Internet and marketing for organizations such as UPS, the Direct Marketing Association (DMA), Business Marketing Association (BMA) and many others. I have co-presented with industry leaders such as Ask Jeeves (currently Ask.com), Symbol Technologies, Avaya, and Microsoft, and have even shared the platform with esteemed industry authors such as Seth Godin. My articles regarding Internet marketing and search engine Technology have been published in both online and offline publications and I am frequently inter-viewed and quoted in articles for prominent business publications, like *Entrepreneur Magazine*.

That said, I've never written a book before, so it remains incumbent upon each of you to write a compelling recommendation of this effort on Amazon. Those inspired to write any sort of negative review - Screw that! Let's see you do any better!

One thing that becomes quite apparent is my fondness for redundancy. There are critical facts and issues which find relevancy within a variety of topics and on a multitude of levels. I can assure you that this is done to help you absorb and retain these essential details and not simply because I love the sound of my writing.

You will notice that I typically pull no punches. I like to think of myself as a shoot from the hip kind of guy, largely because I can't imagine where else one might shoot from…the neck? I'm tired of reading books which curtail the true thoughts of the author because they were afraid of offending someone. My words are not to be taken personally, but rather as a means toward helping your business achieve success within this realm. Take them as cues to fix the flaws that are keeping you from being better.

I'm not ashamed to admit that I've recently become a fan of the show, American Idol, and the reason is Simon Cowell. Mr. Cowell is hard hitting, unbiased and honest. And, it is my opinion, that his professional background gives him the opportunity (and the right) to express himself as an industry expert. All too often, his unfiltered criticism is mistaken for cruelty. Next time you watch the show, give him a closer listen. You'll find that more often than not, he's right on the money and offers the contestants real advice toward becoming better entertainers. Well, in this book, I'm taking my own cue from Mr. Cowell by offering a profoundly honest dialogue – designed specifically to help you.

Me, me, me, me. Okay, enough about me. By this juncture, you're either assuming I know what the hell I'm talking about or just think I'm some sort of ego-inflated ass.

Right on both counts – *let's get started!*

Okay, one more thing about me...although I didn't write it, I swear.

Harry Beckwith, an internationally recognized best selling author, has penned four of my all time favorite books; *Selling the Invisible, What Clients Love, The Invisible Touch and You, Inc.*

If you have not yet read these books, then I implore you to put this one down, get on, Amazon.com, and get them right now! (While you're there, take a minute to write that glowing review we discussed in the previous section.)

Make no mistake; Harry Beckwith changed my life and he can change yours. He has married his remarkable sales and marketing philosophies with a gift for writing and delivered a series of guidebooks toward success in our field.

I continue to implement his practices and wisdom within my own company and use his writings to reinforce my personal success. He remains a true sales/marketing guru and it is my continuing honor to call him a friend.

I f someone asked me what you need to create a superior website, I'd say, "get an Architect from Jersey."

You want not just design – the surface of the building – but architecture – a structure that works wonderfully. And you need a guy from Jersey – no, one specific guy, Larry Bailin – to do it.

Jersey guys want results, and this particular Jersey guy also appreciates that results come from looking the part – from "the package." But Larry also knows that if your package takes two minutes to open, no one will ever get to what's inside.

You will find in this book the no-nonsense, cut-to-the-chase style that those of us living west of New Jersey associate with that region, our stereotypes reinforced by Tony Soprano and others who have flashed across our TVs and movie screens. But Larry is no Wise Guy; he is just a wise fellow, and his wisdom about the most critical new piece of your marketing effort, your website, flows in these pages.

Listen carefully to him. I have, and have prospered from it. Larry wants you to succeed – you can feel it on every page here – and if you read every page here, you will be well on your way.

- Harry Beckwith

1

MOMMY, WHAT WAS THAT NOISE?

Who would have guessed it? A single click was destined to be the greatest innovation in a decade.

Mommy, what was that noise? That was the Internet Billy, that was the Internet.

When Netscape went public over a decade ago, it changed the world forever. In a click heard 'round the world,' a sleepy Internet was primarily used and understood by the technologically gifted (geeks) to talk about things only the technologically gifted (geeks) would talk about (dungeons, dragons, elves and the occasional imaginary girlfriend from Canada.) Additionally, it was certainly well-known to the communications giants who created, maintained and were about to cash in on the infrastructure that is the Internet. No doubt about it…when Netscape went public, the Internet began its rapid ascent toward becoming fully mainstream.

In fact, when news hit that Netscape went public, forty percent of America became instantaneously aware of the Internet's existence, and took immediate steps toward getting online. Now, that's a big noise.

At this point, can you even imagine life without the Internet? I neither can; nor want to. The Internet has truly changed our lives in countless ways, including the manner in which we communicate with peers, colleagues, friends and family. From email, to instant messaging, to VOIP (Voice Over Internet Protocol), the advancements have achieved commonplace status within our homes and businesses. Companies like Vonage, Skype, Comcast, Cablevision and others now offer low cost and even free phone services, with flat monthly rates, by routing your phone calls over the Internet!

I'd like to rant about Instant Messaging for a moment. I actually "IM" people within my own office so I don't have to get up off my keester and walk down the hall to ask a co-worker a quick question. I type it into a little box and boom! Instant answer (not to mention the cool smiley faces you can insert to really get your point across). Does this make me lazy? Ummm, yes, but if you want exercise go buy a fitness book. We're talking about the Internet here. The Internet has taken "lazy" to new level. Hell, we even justify laziness by calling it "productivity" or "efficiency" and I like it! Americans are now the most productively lazy people the world has ever seen!

How about email? I am going to go out on a limb here and say that if you are not using email at this point in time, the rest of us are just waiting for you to die. Anyone that is not using email, especially in their business, will soon just vanish. We won't be able to hear you or communicate with you. You will eventually just cease to be. So, get with the program or move over and let your competition communicate with us in the way we want…the way we demand to be communicated with. Get it? Got it? Good – now go get a friggin' email account.

> *"Friggin'" can be used as an adjective or a verb in New Jersey – it's legal! In another form, you can also use it as a noun, for example, I may tell you to "go frig yourself", and it would be completely acceptable. I love New Jersey!*

Can you even imagine not having email nowadays? I have half a dozen email addresses. I have all of the free ones (Yahoo!, Hotmail, Gmail etc.), an address given to me by my Internet Service Provider, a personal email address, a business address, and now I proudly introduce, *Larry@MommyWhereDoCustomersComeFrom.com*. I receive 200 emails a day at a minimum. Please go ahead and send me one. I will absolutely answer it and I'm looking to break the 400 mark anyway.

Half of the emails I receive are spam. Spam is one of those rare words that were spawned from technology and is actually not an acronym for anything. Spam actually has its origins within a Monty Python skit depicting a restaurant where SPAM® Luncheon Meat, the processed meat in a can, comes with everything you order. No matter what it is, it comes with SPAM. Even if you order SPAM, it comes with SPAM. Still, the other half of my email is of a mission critical nature (a term that has held on from the dot com days). My effectiveness and efficiency is simply far greater with email. Without it my business would suffer because my clients would suffer. And, if my business and clients suffer, then I suffer and if I suffer, I'm bringing everyone else down with me...because I'm just that kind of a guy. I am fairly certain the world would stop spinning without email. Hell, 90% of our politicians use a Blackberry (a nifty device attached to your hip that allows you to send, receive and compose email from anywhere).

According to the April 2006 edition of *Entrepreneur Magazine*, 71% of managers say that email is their primary means of communication. Wow! 71%...think about that and how truly detrimental it would be if you were one of the other 29%.

The way we work, play and shop has changed. The Internet has become ubiquitous (a fancy way to say "omnipresent" when you want to show off your fancy vocabulary skills, but still one of my favorite words to gain popularity in the dot com days) and wraps around all that we do. We pay our bills online, receive money from Internet-connected ATMs and make purchases through web-enabled credit card processing machines. Almost everything touches the Internet at some point. Have you been to a Starbucks lately?

People are routinely using Starbucks as a remote office. On any given day you can see all manners of people with their laptops open, mobile phone head-sets in full effect, conducting business while enjoying a grande half-caf Caramel Macchiato latte with a twist. Starbucks (and now McDonalds) offers their customers high-speed Wi-Fi access (which means "Wireless Fidelity") that allows a wireless Internet connection. It's a great approach that attracts busi-ness people and coffee lovers alike. You can catch me there replying to email, creating one of my famous blog posts or getting out that last minute proposal. Again, I'm the one with the devil-may-care good looks and grande cup o' joe.

Shopping has completely changed. Companies are now in the habit of charging less for services if you book or buy them online. For example, I can rent a car cheaper online than I can if I go to the same company offline. Why? Because the rental car company can save money by making me self-sufficient, and not requiring that I order a car with a car seat from a live (and profoundly more expensive) human being. (By the way, I don't have kids, but sometimes get the car seat anyway. I throw some Cheerios and beer cans in the car seat when I bring it back just to screw with them. Good times.)

The fact is that if you're not comfortable shopping and booking things online, then you better get comfortable spending more money.

Needless to say, the Internet has made quite an impact on the world. In fact, just by writing this chapter, I have a different perspective on the word "noise." I used it in the beginning of my writing as a sound for a single event. Now, I think it's more appropriately used as the descriptor for the background sounds of our lives.

The Internet cannot properly be described as "noise", but more of the "noise" that is everyday life. Still, it creates a question for all those businesspeople wanting to survive.

How can we be heard amongst all that noise?

2

MOMMY, I'M SCARED

Companies that fail to strive for growth inevitably fall behind, shrink, and ultimately die.

I'm going to give you some statistics in this chapter. These statistics represent many different research studies. I read these studies daily and I am always intrigued by the fact that the same study conducted by two different companies always seems to yield differing results. So, in this chapter and throughout the book, I am going to provide averages and approximations instead of just quoting the one source that best supports my argument – fair? Good.

By the time you read this book, it is estimated that over 70% of women in the United States will be online. Women now outnumber men as Internet users. Seventy-five percent of these female Internet users, within the ages of 31 to 40, list the Internet as their preferred purchasing method. Nearly three out of every four people in the US have Internet access at home. That's 204.3 million people or 74.9% of the population above the age of two. (And as soon as Fisher-Price™ comes out with a laptop we'll get those elusive two year olds.)

Approximately 46% of Internet users use online sources when starting the information phase of the buying process for a new item.

On average, fewer than 31% of consumers have never gone online.

People between the ages of 18 and 30 don't know of a world without computers. Those seventeen and younger don't know of, or remember, a world without the Internet.

The Internet touches every business segment on the planet. Let's take a look at the Healthcare industry:

- Roughly eight in ten Internet users saw a medical professional during the past 12 months (80%). Of those, approximately 84% had searched online for health information.

- Senior citizens represent the fastest growing segment of the Internet. According to the U.S. Bureau of the Census and the National Center for Health Statistics, the senior population (those 65 years or older) reached 35 million in 2000, accounting for 12.4% of the U.S. population, which amounts to a 12 percent increase since 1990. The online population for this demographic segment, according to Jupiter Research, was estimated at 4.4 million in 2001, 6.1 million in 2002, 7.6 million in 2003, and is expected to surge to 16.3 million by 2007. This clearly represents a substantial and highly profitable market. The largest year-over-year growth came in 2004, when the population jumped 2.5 million over the 2003 estimate to 10.1 million, and 2005, which accounted for another 2.5 million.

- What about the boomers? Baby boomers (also known as the "sandwich generation") are those born between 1947 and 1964. They accounted for 40.2 million Internet surfers in 2002, 43.3 million in 2003, and will swell to 51.4 million in 2007. Currently, they represent one third of the Internet population, and comprise the largest age group on the Internet.

- Today's boomers will soon become seniors and because of their advanced Internet savvy, their web activity will certainly outperform the current senior class.

Think about how the statements above might impact your business. Do you do business with anyone within these age groups? Do companies you do business with hire people within these age groups? Chances are you've answered "yes" to both. If you're not scared, then you should be. You could be losing more opportunities than you think.

The Internet has changed so much about business and personal life and we're just beginning to experience the early stages of its effects. As far as I'm concerned, the Internet is still in its infancy and the best is yet to come.

When the "Dot Com" bubble burst, people believed that the Internet had become irrelevant – they were wrong. Because of the advancements achieved during the "Dot Com" craze, the Internet actually became stronger than ever. Those companies left standing were now far stronger and had learned the critical rules for success within the new market.

Actually, all the dot com bubble burst did was weed out the businesses that were inherently encumbered by fatal flaws. These businesses would not have been able to survive in any market, and quickly disappeared. During the craze, there was great focus on ideas and little attention paid to the bottom line. Once these entities were asked to make money, they were finished.

The Internet is still growing at break neck speeds. Innovation is thriving and smart businesses and businesspeople are taking full advantage of these innovations. There are more people online, surfing, shopping, researching and making buying decisions than ever before, and this is just the beginning.

No matter your business size, type, or location, the Internet has forever changed the two most important aspects of your business – your customers and your competitors. Your customers are now forward thinking, technologically literate, and maintain broad Internet savvy. They have the world at their fingertips; have no patience for imperfection and even less patience for those wasting their time. They are less forgiving and less brand-loyal than ever before and have become extremely demanding. They have more choices and a seemingly limitless number of companies seeking their business. They are the *new connected* customer and demand that you communicate with them on their terms. These *connected customers* are, without question, the present and future of business.

Your competitor has undergone some major changes as well. Today's business has more competition than at any other time in history. Long distances no longer isolate you from your competitors and, even worse, long distances no longer isolate your customers from your competitors. The Internet has no geographic boundaries. A *connected customer* does not have to get in his car and drive to your three biggest competitors. With a click and a scroll, your *connected customer* is bombarded with hundreds, thousands, and even millions of companies eagerly awaiting the opportunity to earn his or her business. You'd better take action soon because your best customers and potential new ones are now exposed to hungry competitors that you may not have even known existed.

While we are on the topic of competitors, I mentioned Starbucks in the last chapter, but I think it bears repeating. The Wi-Fi access offered by Starbucks is more than just a convenience; it might also be a threat to your business.

You may be saying; "So, you can get on the Internet from Starbucks. Big *friggin'* deal. How is that a threat to my business?"

It is a, "big *friggin* deal!" Here's why: As a salesperson and public speaker, I'm on the road a lot. After I leave an appointment I typically have a small amount of time to kill before my next appointment. I will use the GPS system in my car and find the nearest Starbucks ("if you are in sales you have to get a GPS device, they are amazing!"). Once at Starbucks I order my standard Grande Coffee (just regular coffee, I don't go in for all those frilly fancy coffees and I sure as hell don't use one of those little cardboard cup covers either to protect my hand.) Then I take my seat and break out the laptop. I log onto the Internet, check my email, reply to any urgent messages and get my paperwork started for the client that I have just met.

Does this make me an anal retentive geek? Probably, but it also makes me better than my competition and allows me to offer better service to my customers because I can get things done faster. My clients do not have to wait until I get back to the office to get their projects kicked off or get a reply to an email. In a memorable instance, a potential customer was about to pitch my services in a board meeting, and needed a proposal emailed to him right away. I found the nearest Starbucks, got online and sent the proposal within fifteen minutes of ending our call.

Are you scared yet? If you're my competitor, you'd better be as I will crush you if you let me. I will always adopt the technology that allows me to service my customer better, and be better at it than you are (I stuck my tongue out and made the raspberry noise after typing that sentence).

So, what are the chances that your competitors are sitting next to me at Starbucks, getting a competitive edge on you? There's a damn good chance that they are. So the question becomes—what are you going to do about it? They are striving to be better, stronger and faster than you, and looking to take you're customers. Guess what? If you *don't* do something about it, they will, and it will happen with the simple click of a mouse.

The Starbucks Wi-Fi explosion is just one of the many Internet technologies your competitors are using to crush you and steal your customers. I recently purchased a "Smart Phone." My smart phone is a phenomenal tool for the proactive business person. I am now able to keep my contact list, calendar and to-do's with me at all times. I was able to do this before with my Pocket PC or Palm device, but now, due to a trend called "convergence" (taking multiple devices and making them into one) I have all of these items on my mobile phone. I can look up a contact in my contact manager and call them with the press of a button. I can store thousands of my clients, prospects, and acquaintances as opposed to the hundred or so I could store on my old mobile phone. I can also maintain access to detailed contact information at my fingertips.

Contacts, calendars, and to-do lists alone are not what make my phone "smart." I can now also receive and send email from any location. My phone now retrieves my email for me, and with the small but semi-usable keyboard I can create and reply to any email message. I can download, open, and send attachments. I can even instant message or send a text message, as the need arises. Oh yeah...I can make calls on my smart phone, as well. And when my smart phone drops a call, I can take a picture of myself screaming with my smart phones camera, and send it to my mobile phone carrier. My phone isn't "smart" because of its features. I make it smart by maximizing the phone's feature-set toward better personal efficiency.

How about the truly innovative marketers using technology to better connect with *connected customers*? Do you own an iPod? No? Why not? Not only am I now seeing those white headphones at the gym, but on the subways and trains of New York, airports, buses, and just about everywhere. Did you know that these devices are used for more than just music? I download the latest and greatest sales, marketing and business related audio books in my never-ending attempt to keep myself educated, and again, better than my competition.

Have you heard the term "podcast?" Here is the definition of "podcast" as defined by the "Wikipedia," a free Internet-based encyclopedia.

> "Podcasting" is the distribution of audio or video files, such as radio programs or music videos, over the Internet using either RSS or Atom syndication for listening on mobile devices and personal computers. A podcast is a web feed of audio or video files placed on the Internet for anyone to download or subscribe to. podcaster websites also may offer direct download of their files, but the subscription feed of automatically delivered new content is what distinguishes a podcast from a simple download or real-time streaming. Usually, the podcast features one type of "show" with new episodes either sporadically or at planned intervals such as daily, weekly, etcetera.

The essence of podcasting is about creating content (audio or video) for an audience that wants to listen when they want, where they want, and how they want. They can set their computers to automatically download the latest podcasts to which they've subscribed. Once downloaded, they can take the whole show on the road, or listen from the confines of their computer, all at their own convenience.

Think about the marketing opportunities this offers. Imagine creating a podcast on a subject related to your business. You would essentially be creating your own branded and syndicated radio show. You can create a message that serves two masters. It provides the information your customers want, and the marketing message you need to deliver. Seem far fetched? Think again. Tons of people and businesses are already doing it. All you need is a little inspiration and relevant topics. For example, a financial planner could create a weekly podcast detailing financial trends and other relevant information for their clients and potential clients.

You can even create a video podcast. Imagine you are a real estate agent. You can now create a video podcast about each town in your territory. Potential buyers can view these podcasts and see a tour of local hotspots, culture, schools, homes for sale and they can watch it on the train or from anywhere on the earth. This is just one way businesses are using this technology to gain a competitive advantage.

The long and short of this chapter is simply this: Not keeping up with the changes in new methods of service your customers is a sure ticket to being screwed. These new tools are making your customer's lives easier and saving them money and time, which remains the reason why they will continue to adopt new technologies and methods. Your competitors are utilizing these wonderful tools as well – so where does that leave you?

You took a step in the right direction – you bought this book so you must want to learn what to do, and for that you deserve a pat on the back. If you take only one thing away from this book I hope it's the realization that just sitting around and hoping things will get better will not make it so. You must take action and use your well-honed ability to market your company! Fight back! Get customers and grow your damn business.

For those of you who think everything is just peachy with your business, then think about this. Walt Whitman once said, "Even if you're on the right track, unless you keep moving you're still going to get hit by the train."

FDR once said, "The only thing to fear is fear itself." Personally I don't fear fear. I fear bankruptcy, losing my business, not being able to pay my employees and having to find a real job. I will always look at how to better connect with my customers and I implore you to do the same.

3

MOMMY, WHY CAN'T I MAKE FRIENDS?

Mommy, why can't I make friends?

I promise that you'll make friends. You're just looking in the wrong places.

It's easy for me to tout the benefits of the Internet and how to be in touch with customers because I've been doing it for years. I'm what they call an "early adopter." There are many classifications of technology users and I'm one of those types that seem to be enthralled by technology. Thus, according to a book by Geoffrey A. Moore called, *Crossing the Chasm*, I am an "early adopter." I seek out and use technology, gadgets, and software to its fullest capacity. As one of these "early adopters," I also spend a good deal of money toward satisfying my cravings for newer and better gear. Thank God for eBay!

Now, I realize that the majority of you are not early adopters, so I'm going to let you in on one of our secrets. If spending a little money on technology allows you to be faster and more efficient, it's probably worth it – even if it's only a few minutes a day. As the old saying goes, "time is money." Remember, if you can save time you can certainly make more money.

So, it's time to let me help you lower the noise, take a look at the manner in which people find products and services on the Internet, and the ways they interact with the tools used in the process.

We've discussed iPods, smart phones and WiFi, but we really need to focus on search engines, which are one of the major vehicles used by the masses to find your company. Close to 80% of Internet users utilize search engines to research, locate, and purchase products and services. Notice that I said "products and services" – and not just products. If you haven't noticed then you're not paying attention, and it's possible that your ADD has kicked in. ADD needs to be treated because it will keep you from…
Oh Look! A bunny!

My company maintains over 400 web pages in major search engines. Fully 90% of my customers are service companies, and do not sell anything online, but themselves. They have no shopping engines, "buy now" buttons, or PayPal interfaces. They attract those looking for their services, and not necessarily products. My client base consists of manufacturers, distributors, and professional service providers such as lawyers, doctors, and real estate agents. Many of my clients sell products via e-commerce shopping engines as well. Search engines can help both types of businesses attract and retain customers. Still, I want to be clear that selling products online and success-fully converting clients are not synonymous. Plenty of service-oriented companies have become very profitable, online marketers.

The moral of this story is that no matter what product or service you offer, there are potential customers out there looking for what you have to offer. I have yet to find a business that could not benefit from being online. To steal a line from the X-Files – "They're out there" – so you need to be out there too!

Where was I? Oh right! Search engines. There are roughly a dozen or so search engines that are considered "major search engines", but most people can name five. These twelve search engines account for about 95% of all searches done online. At some point, you're likely to get contacted by a company offering to register you with thousands of online search engines. Don't bite. Remember, it's about quality, not quantity. You need to focus on the primary search engines, such as Google, MSN, and Yahoo. These are the engines that will get you customers. It does you no good to be number one on an unknown, unused search engine. Unless we're talking about insurance, don't pay for something you'll never use.

Currently, the major mainstream search engines are as follows: MSN Search, Yahoo!, Google, AOL Search, Ask.com (formerly Ask Jeeves), Teoma, All the Web, Lycos, AltaVista, HotBot, Netscape A9 and Looksmart.

I define "major search engines" as being those most popular with the masses. These search engines account for roughly 98% of all searches performed on the Internet. Now, things change very quickly when it comes to the Internet and search engines. A new kid on the block could easily create a following and challenge the giants. Still, for now, the giants stand alone, as listed.

Search engines are the primary source of leads when it comes to the Internet. There are other ways to attract customers, such as email, blogs, etc., and I will get to some of these methods in a later chapter, but for now, let's focus on the primary vehicle – search engines.

Those using search engines in their online quests for products and services have gotten very savvy when it comes to searching. Google recently released an interesting statistic. They stated that searchers typically use a three to five word phrase when performing a search. This is a huge behavioral change from years ago when searchers used to use "keywords", or single words, to perform a search. When this method generated irrelevant or overwhelming numbers of results, users refined their search by adding more keywords to the query.

Today, searchers just type in the grouped key phrases all at once, or in three to five word phrases. Thus, single keywords have actually evolved into key phrases. When you think about it, this is a pretty amazing phenomenon. In actuality, it's more a behavioral evolution. The Internet continues to grow at an astounding rate. In fact, back in the mid to late 90's the Internet doubled in size every 90 days, and searchers were being faced with more and more websites from which to choose. As such, it became increasingly difficult to sift through page after page of often irrelevant search results. So, what happened? The searchers evolved, got smarter and began to adapt to the still developing search engines. The more specific the search, the more accurate the results. Simple.

After reading the last couple of paragraphs you should have noticed something. People are adapting (it's what people do). They are changing their behavior in concert with the growth and development of the Internet. Think about that for a minute. What are the implications to your business? Change is a fact of life. John F. Kennedy once said, "Change is the law of life. And those who look only to the past or present are certain to miss the future." Your customers are evolving faster than ever. Widespread customer behavioral changes used to take many years. The Internet has accelerated these changes by at least a hundred fold. You need to keep up with changes and as President Kennedy said, "you must look to and embrace the future."

If you have a website and are not focusing on search engines to attract customers, you are simply making a fatal mistake. You can have the most technically advanced site in the world, but if no one knows you exist, you've got nothing. The need to address search engines as part of your overall marketing strategy is absolutely critical. Search engines will produce qualified potential customers looking for your products and services.

I challenge you to perform a search in a major engine in the exact manner as a potential customer. What three to five word phrase would be used by someone interested in your offerings? Who shows up? Is it you? Probably not. Look at the search results. Do you know what you're looking at? Competitors! *Competitors attracting your customers and closing business that should be yours.*

4

MOMMY, SOMEONE'S AT THE DOOR

Connecting with a *connected customer.*

Selling online to a *connected customer* is not much different than selling to someone through traditional means. Sales basics still apply. An online sale requires the same amount of attention as an offline sale. While the absence of a face-to-face experience can create some unique issues, these are easily overcome with proper planning. Sales gurus like Harry Beckwith, Brian Tracy, and Neil Rackham can make you a better salesperson. My job is to help you examine the distinct challenges presented by the web, and assist you in negotiating your way around the common mistakes. Remember that qualified leads live and die in an instant on the Internet. Start treating them as such.

Online and offline customers demand the same level of customer service. In fact, because an online consumer does not have the comfort of a personal experience, a little more "virtual handholding" is often required. Before you actually start selling to the *connected customer*, they must first be persuaded into an initial contact. Those without ecommerce shopping engines on their websites will typically be contacted in one of three ways: A phone call (usually during business hours) an occasional email, or a request created from a structured form residing on the site. When sending information, *connected customers* tend to prefer the use of forms as opposed to unstructured email, but only if it's easy. A well-constructed contact form is a must for your site.

One of the first things I look at when evaluating a website is the contact information. There are certain conventions that *connected customers* look for when navigating through a page. One of these conventions is a link or button titled, "Contact." Not "Call Us," "Request Information," or some other variation. You need to use the word "contact," as it's become a web standard.

One of the most common mistakes is that typical contact forms (if there is one); require the visitor to answer too many questions. You don't typically need a lot of information and most people will not feel comfortable filling out a long detailed form before they are sure you can help them. I always ask a new client about the sales process that occurs after they receive a new request via form. Nine times out of ten, they tell me that they are going to call the potential customer. Then why make them fill out all that information when you can gather those details over the phone in a more personal way? Asking questions is one of the major keys to successful selling and rapport building, so why waste it on a form? Make it as easy as possible for a potential customer to make contact, even if it makes your job a little harder. For example, why ask for city, state and zip code? Why not just zip code? If you have their zip code you can easily look up the city and state. This eliminates two fields right off the bat.

Do you see where I'm going with this? It's about the customer. It's about making them feel comfortable and persuading them to make contact. Start looking at your website as a selling tool, because that's exactly what it is. It's a "persuasion vehicle", and you need to be adept at persuading the right customers to move forward while nicely encouraging the wrong ones to leave. Managed properly, the web can do a great deal for you and your business. The web can help you convert those with passing interest into customers, while assisting you in filtering out bad leads. The right message should persuade the right customers to do business, while dissuading those not truly candidates for your products and services. This helps prevent a poor customer experience, and garners their respect for your business. Bottom line? A well constructed website will help you get customers, and that's what it's all about.

Believe it or not, your website can generate a significant amount of revenue. You just have to remember that old adage – "You have to spend money to make money." Don't cheap out! I'm not saying you have to dump a ridiculous amount of money into this venture. I am saying that your decision cannot be solely motivated by the price of going forward. Great websites are developed by great companies maintaining the expertise to address the requirements of your business, while successfully targeting the needs of your customers. Their value cannot be underestimated.

Since we are on the subject of web development companies, let's elaborate (and rant), a bit. Technical proficiency alone does not make a web developer. I'm proficient enough in the kitchen to make dinner, but that does not make me a chef.

Websites are sales and marketing tools. Period. The technical skill required to build one is quite secondary. Most of the web developers out there (you can throw a rock out of your window and probably hit one) are not marketers. They typically don't look at the sales and marketing fundamentals, or create measurable strategies when developing websites.

Your basic website developer is very adept and proficient in building the physical site, but can often miss the mark when asked to design what you really need.

Now, don't get me wrong. I have a great deal of respect and admiration for the work of a talented programmer. However, from a business perspective, it's your responsibility to understand their limitations. Take a look at their work from both a business and design perspective. Look at the ease of use on a site. Read the content. Know what the website offers. Does it convey the right message to persuade a visitor with related needs? Does the developer know what impact the website had on their client's business? Did the developer integrate a sound marketing structure into the website? It's okay if the developer only created the physical site. There is nothing wrong with that. If you are comfortable with their technical expertise, and have confidence in their ability to deliver the right kind of product, they should probably be hired. Still, you might want to see if they have an Internet marketing partner to assist in developing the usability, content, and overall marketing approach of the site.

When you ask your developer about Internet marketing and the answer resembles anything even close to "we can do that, all we have to do is put keywords on your site", run for the hills. I'll explain why keywords don't work in a later chapter.

From a technical perspective, web development requires skill, but creating a proper, successful, online sales and marketing strategy requires a different brand of expertise. Going into this project with one and not the other is a guaranteed recipe for failure.

On the flip side let's examine ad agencies and design firms (I just stretched out my arms and inter-laced fingers, palms facing forward, and cracked my knuckles to prepare for this rant.) They are another group proclaiming great website development profi-ciency. Some of the most talented and creative people I've ever met have been the designers and principals from ad agencies and design firms. I have seen some creative work that has truly blown me away! Being a classically trained artist I have a finely tuned appreciation for creativity, and those with the imagination and vision to create compelling design. Being an entrepreneur, I have a great admiration for anyone that can use those skills to create revenue for their clients.

Ad agencies and design firms can often (I said "can") let creativity get in the way of creating a revenue driven website. All too often, I am asked to evaluate an ad agency-developed website only to find that creative elements have blocked the site's ability to communicate the message. I meet with a lot of ad agencies and design firms, who rarely fail to mention how many awards they have won for creativity. They never tell me how many customers their creativity has won for their clients. Why is that? Wouldn't it be refreshing for an ad agency or design firm to come into your office, and instead of showing you a list of their awards, provide a list of customers their creativity has won for their clients?

Let me tell you why most ad agencies focus on the creative – lack of sales skills (there I said it). Many agencies reluctantly admit to an inadequate understanding of basic sales processes. They do not educate themselves on selling styles, techniques and innovations. They don't read sales books or attend sales seminars. Why is this a big deal? Well…what the hell is the goal of marketing? Acquisition of customers, right? If you agree with this premise, then you must also agree that marketing exists to *sell*. There must be a sales process component to the marketing campaign. An ad agency must design their creative elements to sell. If you hire an agency pushing the value of creative concepts as opposed to genuine selling mechanisms, you'll get what you pay for. Pretty pictures – and nothing more.

Shame on all those ad agencies and design firms who are promoting their marketing prominence while consistently failing to develop any sales expertise. Marketing and sales simply go hand in hand. How can you create successful marketing programs without understanding sales? One without the other is like Corn Flakes without the milk! I love the pretty pictures, but these guys are doing a half-assed job.

Some ad agencies and design firms are not comfortable with their clients marketing on the web. Some firms are actually scared of losing offline budgets, so they shy away from mentioning or supporting online marketing efforts. Again, if they say, "we'll put keywords on your site," you know what to do.

Design is not subjective. Design exists for one reason – to persuade customers. Every element, graphic, link, and line of text should accomplish the following:

1. **It should make you look professional.** There's no gray area. You either look professional, or you don't.

2. **Reinforce your brand.** Branding is such an overused word. I've seen it abused so often it seems to have lost meaning. Anything that does not make the company money seems to fall into the branding category. True branding is wrapped around revenue generating marketing efforts. If these efforts don't make money that's okay; just don't call it branding. There are no guarantees in marketing, and certain things might not work. Your website should be consistent with other forms of marketing. Your brochures, business cards, print ads and writing styles should all follow a theme. The site content should portray your corporate personality.

3. **Reduce bad leads.** If your website has the right message, it should dissuade the wrong people from contacting you. Bad leads waste time. If your web message is producing leads you can't service, then it needs to be changed.

4. **Convert those with interest into success.** Success may be the purchase of a product through your e-commerce shopping engine, the download of a white paper, or to simply make contact. It truly depends on your specific business type. I mentioned this earlier. A web lead is a sale more easily lost than won. (Think about that; it might be profound, but I'm not sure.) If you're being contacted by someone with a need, think about the process that brought them to you. This person did a web search, clicked on your listing (out of millions of choices), visited your website, read your material, and made contact with you – that's a pretty qualified lead. Now the only thing you can do is screw it up!

5. **Get you customers.** The greatest value a properly designed, developed, and marketed website can provide is the ability to get you customers. I guarantee that no matter what type of business you have, this can be achieved. Pig farmers, Laundromat owners, or Fortune 500 CEOs can all realize the same goals. Right now, potential customers are searching for your products. If they're not finding you – they've likely found someone else.

If you are looking to create a website long on bells and whistles, but short on substance, then you're making a great big, but very common mistake (Please don't do that – it makes me sad). Folks, when it comes to the web – less is the new more. Simple wins out against complex. At the risk of being redundant (but writing a bigger book), design is not subjective, and exists only to persuade customers! Websites should not be marketing department eye candy. Those days are over! Flash intros on business websites should be illegal! They just slow down the site and keep your customers from accessing the information they seek.

Did you know that on average, "skip intro" links are clicked on in about a tenth of a second? With this in mind, think about who you are really developing that fancy flash intro for. I'll tell you who. You! There I said it, and I'm glad I said it. You did it for you! Now you can say that you have a cool website. Look at all the animation (he said sarcastically in a whiney voice). Look at the spinning! Look at all the colors! Keep watching, some sort of something or other is going to fly out from the top and explode into a rainbow of pretty colors! Blah…blah…blah. GAG! You make me sick! I bet your friends also told you it's a great website. Remember something – your friends are not your customers. Unlike your customers, you're not at risk of losing your friends to the gigantic list of potential suppliers on Google. If you can't quickly prove to a customer that you're a candidate to service their needs, they'll return to that gigantic list of your competitors with one swift click of the back button. Stop with the flash intros, the music, the animation, and the sounds. People just want to find what they need. They did not come to your site to be entertained. If you want to entertain people, learn to play guitar.

Oh! Did you know that roughly sixty plus percent of Internet users surf the web from work? That's right. Sixty percent of your employees are probably doing it, right now. Need proof? In March 2006, ComScore Networks served 700,000 streams of NCAA Men's College Basketball finals. Seventy-three percent of these streams were served to workers in an office. The

April 2006 issue of Entrepreneur Magazine noted that 23% of corporate email is unrelated to work.

So what is the effect of putting music or sound on your site? If I'm online at work, and surfing for personal reasons, I'm outta there the moment any music starts playing. And, I promise you – I'm not alone. Do you want to chase 60% of internet users away from your site? Go ahead and hire the band.

This chapter is long for a reason. This is important. Too many businesses make poor decisions when it comes to their websites and need to understand that a good website is not solely design, programming, or marketing – it's all three.

This chapter is about selling to a *connected customer*. Selling to the *connected customer* is less about your personal sales skills, and more about the selling power of your website. It's a partnership. Your website has to sell you and you have to sell your offerings. The website tees it up, and you drive it down the fairway. Your website throws out the bait, and you reel it in. You smell what I'm cooking?

To all web developers, ad agencies, marketers and design firms. I am making generalizations in this chapter. I do not mean to say that ALL firms are poor and especially not yours – you rock! It's all the other firms that suck.

5

MOMMY, CAN I GO OUT AND PLAY?

Are you ready to play with the masses? How's your message? How are your touch points?

Potential customers are out there right now looking for your products and services. I keep repeating this throughout this book because it's the single most important detail that drives everything you do online. Before you can even think about interacting with, selling, or marketing to these *imminent buyers*, you have to make sure that you are ready.

In this chapter we are going to look at your "touch points." How are your points of contact? Is everything a potential customer interacts with perfect? Based on the sad state of customer service in this country, chances are that your service is poor, but let's assume that you are better than most. This makes you, at best, average. Everyone can raise the bar when it comes to improving your customer touch points. When you look at your online touch points, where do you think you need work? When was the last time you looked at your website's touch points?

I mentioned earlier that an online lead is a sale to lose. If your website, message, or any other touch point fails, you will not even get a chance to speak to that potential customer. You are more than likely (if you're in the group of average marketers) losing potential opportunities everyday.

When taking on a new client, part of my company's process is to mystery shop their site. This often involves making a purchase, and evaluating the follow-up process. However, when measuring a potential business-to-business client without an online sales presence, we make contact. We either send an email or fill out any existing contact form. We submit qualified questions, in the manner of a qualified customer.

You may be surprised (although, I'm not) to learn that 8 out of every 10 of these mystery shopping exercises fail miserably. We've received errors when we submitted forms. When presented to the client, this is typically met with true surprise, or an embarrassed excuse. More often than not, we actually get no response from our requests. How absurd is that? A potential, fairly well-qualified customer makes contact with you and receives no immediate response? Insanity! Another ridiculous excuse to the lack of response issue is, "I'm not even sure who gets those forms." *What?* Are you out of your mind? It often turns out that those responsible for following-up no longer work for the company – Ughhhh! This stuff drives me absolutely nuts! I've noticed that companies failing to respond to our mystery shop requests also tend to complain about business being slow, that marketing does not work, and think their industry is going to the dogs – go figure.

To prevent me from having to come over there and beat you, there are some very simple processes one can put in place to avoid losing a potential sale. Now, someone usually starts off the work day by checking phone messages and emails. This is a standard routine in most offices. So why not modify the process? Boot up the computer, turn on the lights, make some coffee, check phone messages, and check email. Okay – here comes the new task. Go to your website and send yourself an email, just as a customer would. Fill out the form, if you have one. Make sure the form request is received, and you'll be ready to start the day.

Test your touch points everyday. Make this someone's job. A short, simple test may be just the thing to make you lots of money. Who knows? You might get a request from your soon-to-be largest client!

I like to take things to the next level because I'm a stickler for process. A critical part of every process in my office is accountability. So, I would also ask the person checking the form to put the received copy on my desk each day. By making it mandatory, I get to see the results of the daily tests, and I'm insuring that it gets done. At the very least, I receive one lead through my website per day. Because I refuse to forfeit even one lead, I am going to make sure that all bases are covered. Some of the leads I've gotten through my website have been Fortune-sized companies. Do you want to risk losing accounts like these? I don't – and I won't.

Before I end this chapter, there is something that bears repeating. If your website has done its job, you should be receiving qualified leads. As such, it is incumbent upon you to be on top of your sales game, and turn those qualified leads into customers. This means that you need to be just as polished as your site. All your sales ducks need to be in a row. You have to have great, and I mean perfect, follow-up skills. You need to know how to sell. Keep in mind that if someone is contacting you on the Internet they have probably also contacted at least two other companies. Your Internet marketing company, ad agency, design firm and web developer cannot close deals for you. You are solely responsible for this task. If you screw it up, it really is your fault. If the marketing worked, and the sale didn't, then it's time to start some sales training. Remember, without one, the other will soon fail.

I have two examples which illustrate the importance of a strong sales process. One is a personal experience, and one involves a major sales failure on the part of one of my clients.

Example 1: About two years ago my company moved into new offices. This office is at least eight times larger than our old office (life is good) and we needed a new phone system to support the additional space and people. We also have remote users, and wanted to utilize some of the benefits VOIP (Voice Over Internet Protocol) provides. This includes allowing our remote users to have phones in their home office which seamlessly integrates with our main systems.

I went online as a well-educated and qualified *imminent buyer* (remember that I'm an early adopter and was well educated on VOIP). I located three local companies that looked like they may be able to help me. I filled out two forms and called the third. Guess how many called me back? One. Guess who got the sale. The other two lost a good-sized deal. Since purchasing this phone system, we have made a point of recommending it to others, and created more business for our service provider. However, the other two companies did put me on their email list without permission.

Example 2: An *imminent buyer* does a web search and finds a website that looks as though it's run by a suitable provider. A form is filled out and, within the same business day, a salesperson from the company calls the potential customer to offer some assistance. So far, so good. Right? Right. In fact, a deal is made. The *imminent buyer* wants to buy some products, as a trial. If the products work out, they will agree to buy them for the entire company on an on-going basis. There are over 800 people in this office, and this represents a substantial opportunity. However, they need the products within 24 hours, and specifically make this clear to the salesperson. The salesperson acknowledges the need, and promises the customer next business day delivery.

Well, the next day arrives, but the product does not. The buyer checks the tracking number online, only to find out that the product did not leave as scheduled, and was sent via ground freight. Given these details, the *imminent buyer* is now livid, and is officially a lost sale. So angry was this customer that he fired off one of the nastiest emails I've ever encountered, which detailed the failure to pay attention, and resulted in the loss of an extremely valuable customer.

The *imminent buyer* was Pixar Animation Studios. *Ouch.*

Message

Your message is absolutely the most important thing to address. Your message will be at the forefront of all your marketing. In order to create the proper message (at least when it comes to the Internet), you need to understand your customers and their needs. Here is a little tip I give in my presentations to help people evaluate their online message.

WWW – Prior to reading this book you associated this acronym with World Wide Web. Replace that definition with this one:

> *Who is your customer?*
> *What do they want?*
> *Where do they get it?*

Who is your customer? Do you know who your customer is? Their average age, demographic, professional position, industries they serve, unique market challenges, new business objectives, changes within their industry, etc. This is *very* important. If you don't understand who your customer is, you cannot possibly create a compelling message.

Ask this question of every employee with access to potential customers, and you'll get many different answers. Everyone in the company should have a unified view of your customers. Once you and your employees have developed a cohesive view of your customers, you will be ready to move on to the next "W."

What do they want? What does your customer want, in relation to what you offer? If you know what your customer wants, look at your website from that point of view, and see if a visiting potential customer can determine your relevant offerings within 8-10 seconds. Knowing exactly what your customers want will help you to craft a message that immediately captures their attention.

Where do they get it? Where does your customer go next? They land on your website and identify that you may be able to help them. Is it clear where they should go next? This is classified as a "call to action." Is there a clear call to action on your website? Will a visitor be frustrated trying to find information about a specific product or service? Even worse, will they not be able to easily find contact information should they need to speak with someone? The process of converting an interested visitor into a customer is obviously the key to your overall success. A *great* call to action should be crystal clear and in their face.

With the three W's covered, you can now create your message.

Step 1 ■ Start to think like your customers. You and your customers likely view your services in differing manners. When people have a need and go online to find answers, they are rarely seeking a specific solution. More often, they will search the problem, not the desired solution. When they get to your website, they will be looking for language that addresses their needs. If you think about it, it makes sense.

If I needed a program to help my company manage financials, I would search for "accounting software" and not the brand name of the program. Along the same lines, if I end up on a software company's website and the link reads, "Accounting Software", that's what I'm clicking on. If the link only reads "Peachtree" or "QuickBooks", there's a good chance that a less-informed customer might be left confused. To make a better connection with a *connected customer* you need to be disconnected. This means being disconnected from industry jargon and buzz-words. Think like a customer.

Now that we have covered touch points and messages, let's take a look at the effects produced by your web design. You must ensure that all of the elements of your website provide a clear direction for your visitor. Is your website functional from a business perspective? Is it easy to navigate? Does it load fast? Does it work with the technology your visitors are using?

Ease of navigation is the most important element of a great website. It is also the most important thing to a visitor. Think about your own online experiences. Do you want to use a website that makes it hard to find what you are looking for? Of course you don't! (If you do, email me, and I'll send you a huge list of terrible websites.) Neither does your customer. When was the last time you took a good hard look at your website to find ways to make it easier to navigate? I'll bet we can all come up with ways to improve your website's ease of use – why haven't you?

What makes a website easy to navigate? Two things. First, you need to reduce the number of clicks it takes for visitors to access their desired information. Look at your website and see if there are any clicks that can be eliminated. An example of this would be in the Flash intro's "skip intro" button. This is a useless click that prevents someone from getting to the information they want. Another example (also a Flash example) is having someone choose whether they want to view the website in Flash or HTML format. You can use technology to determine if someone has Flash installed and automatically switch to the best available option.

The second thing that leads to better navigation is redundancy. Redundancy, redundancy, redundancy. Your website is one place where you can be obscenely redundant and not annoy anyone. If you put ten people in a room, and had each of them interact with the same website, chances are they would all do it differently. Some would read more than others. These people might click on text-based links more than navigation buttons. Then, you have the skimmers. A skimmer is looking for the next page within 8 to 10 seconds of arriving on your site. Some may read all of the content on your site, and click on the links that are (or should be) waiting for them at the bottom of each page. The text links residing at the bottom of the page are called *redundant text links*. In the end, there should be many ways to get to the same information if you want your site to be user-friendly for everyone.

In a later chapter, I'll provide more detail regarding things you can do to create easier site navigation. For now, let's press on – we've got a lot to cover.

How about load times? Does the speed in which your website loads play a part in your website's ease of use? Damn right it does! The slower your website is, the harder it is to use...*especially* for those using dial up connections. You may think that everyone has access to a high-speed Internet connection – not so. Roughly 50% of American Internet users have high-speed connections. While that's a lot of people, remember that 50% of American users are still dialing up. Slow connections are not just limited to home users either. Many businesses are in areas where high-speed is not readily available. Make sure your site loads in a maximum of five to six seconds using a dial up connection. Test it yourself, and see just how long five to six seconds actually is when you're staring at your computer monitor.

Hard to read equals hard to use. The content on your website says a lot about your company, products, and services. You must create content that is pointed and professional. Do not take the same content from your brochure and paste it into your website. A website and brochure have two totally different audiences. Active versus Passive. I mentioned this before. Print media is passive and your website is active.

Do not write content solely for the purpose of showing up in a search engine. This is a very flawed tactic. You end up with content that reads like it was written by Rain Man. *Would you like to buy a Buick? It's time to buy a Buick. If you're looking for a Buick we've got a Buick. I drive a Buick, yeah, definitely drive a Buick. Drive a Buick, up and down the driveway you can drive a Buick. Would you like to buy a Buick? Click here to buy your Buick.* There are some companies that tout their ability to help you show up in search engines, but will compromise your content with exactly this sort of drivel. You might show up in the search engine, but no one will make contact.

Remember, the goal is not to show up in a search engine. I know this is a book about Internet marketing, but the goal is still to increase sales. The goal is to increase revenues by turning those with passing interest into customers. This can only be achieved by developing your site for customers, not search engines. Try not to lose sight of this objective. If you create a powerful site, filled with useful information for your potential customers, the search engine placement will follow.

Develop meaningful content that helps convince a visitor of your value. Written well, your content will instill confidence in visitors, and persuade them to make contact. A good Internet marketing consultant can help you write copy that persuades a potential customer, while generating positive search engine placement. Remember that placement alone produces no return – you must have a solid and complete strategy that includes clear and concise content. Hire a professional to develop persuasive copy. It will make your life easier and it's well worth the money.

My rules and views on website usability may differ from those of other writers and experts. You don't need to understand all of the rules of usability. Just use common sense. Try to look at your site objectively. Try to look at things from your customer's point of view. Have friends and family look at your site and get some impartial opinions. Ask them to keep the opinions focused on the usability and message of the website, as opposed to design, because everyone will have their own opinion regarding the way it looks. If you choose a good firm to help you with the plan, one that knows all the intricate rules about website usability, then your design should be inline with the goals of the site.

People are quick to remember the most useful sites, not simply the most creative. Quickly, what was the most creative website you've visited in the last 30 days? Most people cannot answer this question because the creative elements blocked the communication. I'll bet you can name your favorite site. The answer most often turns out to be a useful site with minimal design components. People don't remember the design; they remember the experience.

Everything on your website should have a reason for being there. If it does not, get rid of it or replace it with something that will either persuade your visitor, or make your site easier to use. Ideally, it should do both.

Here's my number one rule when it comes to website usability: *You must make it easier for a visitor to move forward than back.* With a click or two of the back button, your potential customers can easily go back to a gigantic list of your competitors. And then... you're history.

6

MOMMY, MAKE ME A PROMISE

There are no guarantees.

Are you one of those people that will make a buying decision based on a guarantee? A lot of people base their purchases on this alone and, as a result, many companies put more into their guarantees than the actual value of the product or service. Ironically, top quality products and services are rarely known for their guarantee. For example, Mercedes-Benz does not offer a 100,000-mile warranty like some other car manufacturers. Why? Because people that buy a Mercedes know they are purchasing a quality vehicle, and the warranty would do little to persuade them into making a purchase.

I recently found my all-time favorite guarantee printed on the side of my friendly neighborhood garbage truck. It reads, "Satisfaction Guaranteed or Double your Garbage Back." Perfect! Finally, a guarantee that puts things in perspective! Most guarantees (at least the ones that are Internet marketing related) do indeed give you "double your garbage back" in the form of aggravation and extra work. Not only will it put you twice as far behind your competition, it will also double the amount of time required to get your project up and properly running. On the bright side, if you're lucky, you may even get some of your misspent money back, but I "guarantee" it will take twice as long as it did for you to dole it out in the first place.

Services are the same as products when it comes to guarantees – the best services don't need one. A guarantee is nothing more than an excuse to fail, providing a "safety net" for the service provider. The worst part is that the safety net usually ends up costing you far more than the security you gain by having it. Chris Farley said it best in the movie "Tommy Boy." He played lovable Tommy Callahan, a rookie road warrior (a term given to on-the-road-sales-people), selling brake pads. When faced with selling his non-guaranteed brake pads against a competitor's guaranteed product, he made the point that the product has a guarantee because the product needs a guarantee. He eloquently stated to his prospect, "what you really have there is a guaranteed piece of $!@#. If you'd like me to take a dump in a box and mark it 'guaranteed,' I will. I've got spare time."

The Internet marketing industry is notorious for providing empty guarantees. As we all know, life and business really have no guarantees, and this certainly applies to marketing of any kind. There is always a risk associated with marketing. As business people dedicated to growing our businesses, we try to mitigate these risks with facts, reputation, track record and measurability. We are all inundated with spam promising "Guaranteed Placement in Google," and "Top Search Engine Rankings Guaranteed!" Still, until you receive a personal pledge of top positioning from the Google company founders, you'll find these promises more than likely to be an excuse to fail, rather than a guarantee of success.

What do I mean by "Excuse to fail?" That's a great question, and I'm glad I asked. Let's examine a typical Internet marketing guarantee. First and foremost, there is always a placement and/or positioning guarantee statement that will read something similar to "Top ten placements – guaranteed or your money back." This is your first major red flag. No one can guarantee placement — period! Even Google specifically warns about companies that guarantee placement. For more information on this, visit their "Fact and Fiction" page at `http://www.google.com/webmasters/seo.html`.

Typically, this type of money-back guarantee will cost you more in the long run. You may be asking, "What do

I have to lose if I get my money back?" That's another great question, and I'm glad I asked. How about lost opportunity and time? Internet marketing is a phenomenal and effective way to attract potential customers at their exact time of need. After all, a visitor to your site is almost always looking for your exact product or service. If the company you hire to implement your Internet marketing initiatives fails, you have your "guarantee," but what does it get you? You already missed opportunities to capture great potential customers, who just ended up on your competitor's doorstep.

Now what? Not only do you have to collect on your "guarantee" (good luck with that), you now have to start all over again, researching Internet marketing consultants, setting up meetings, reading proposals and providing support and information. How much time does that take and what does it cost you in money, manpower, and lost opportunities? Remember that little phrase, "double your garbage back?" Bingo! Time to do it all over again. Still, it's okay…you've gotten your money back from the last company that failed, right?

I'm going to say this once again: there are no guarantees in business. Choose a service based on a sterling reputation rather than a hollow guarantee. Research references and the track record of the company you are hiring. You're trusting them to help you succeed. If you pass on a great company just so you can have your nice warm security blanket, then shame on you. Great marketers do not have guarantees because, like Mercedes Benz, they don't need them. Do you really want your money back or do you want the program to succeed? You need a company committed to your genuine long-term success, not some overly-hyped benchmark.

Since we mentioned benchmarks, let's talk about "performance based guarantees" for a moment. Performance based guarantees are given by companies that get paid when they deliver results. Sounds too good to be true, right? Well, you know what they say about something sounding "too good to be true." Let me tell you a quick story about a woman I once interviewed. She worked for one of these "Pay for Performance" Internet marketing companies, and recently found herself unemployed because they went out of business. She told me about their "Pay for Performance" model. "We only got paid when we achieved results for our clients. Most of our clients were not worth any long-term effort. If we couldn't produce huge volume for them right away, we ignored their programs and focused on the clients we could make quick money on."

That's the mindset in a nutshell. Pay for Performance companies chase the money – period! Can you blame them? That's the trade off you allow by not taking on any personal risk. You can't expect companies that are performance-based or guarantee-driven to treat your project with personal accountability, because they haven't any. They are accountable to the guarantee only, and if they don't meet the **guarantee** or benchmark, it's no big deal – they can always give you back your money…eventually.

7

MOMMY, I KNOW MY ABC'S

A quick look at some of the basics.

With all of the features you can incorporate into your website, it's very easy to forget about some of the basics. We've already talked about ease of use and load times. Let's also review some of the rules to creating better connections with your web customers.

Did you know that each website visitor interacts with the site in their own specific way? It's true. There is a pattern to which the eyes of your visitors scan information on a website. Understanding this information will enable you to properly lay out your site, while making it easier for your visitors to find their information. How's that for a win-win?

There are numerous studies and tracking methods used to evaluate and interpret website activity. These methods vary in terms of focus groups, interviews and even technological methods. In some tests, users actually wear cameras to physically capture the "hot spots" on a website. This is also a method used to determine "dwell times," which show how long website visitors linger in certain areas of a website – pretty sweet (sweet is the new cool. Cool still remains cool, but sweet is also cool.)

These studies provide very useful information. One actually determined that there are areas of a website which are nearly invisible to a user. These studies were conducted by putting nonsensical information in various quadrants of popular websites, just to determine a reaction from the visitors. Results from this particular study concluded that the upper left hand side and lower right hand side are the least effective areas to attract a user's attention. Interesting? Maybe.

While certainly intriguing, the findings were not conclusive enough to create a standard for proper website design.

Most studies fail to be conclusive enough to create a standard. Since there are no standards in website development and design, most sites will produce differing eye movement behavior in each visitor. You simply cannot take the results from one website and use them on another of completely different design, and containing dissimilar information. The individual user certainly factors into the equation. Each person maintains unique needs, goals and skill levels. I've read hundreds of usability studies and they all produce slightly different results. However I've found that the majority seem to agree on the basics. As such, I have been able to gather a comprehensive approach to "good practices."

I'm going to outline a summary of my own standards and good practices. I've used my personal training and client experiences to provide a baseline of understanding the manner in which a visitor's eyes track across a website. Please remember there is no gospel of usability. My standards reflect my experience, and you're welcome to use these "good practices" that have worked so well for my clients.

To begin, it appears to be rigidly common behavior for all users to scan about a site, as opposed to dwelling in a particular section. This tends to mirror other studies and statistics regarding the amount of time one typically spends on a page before navigating away. Understanding the manner in which a visitor scans the elements of your site enables you to create a more powerful design.

Let's review how to use text on your website. Smaller font sizes seem to promote deeper focus, while larger fonts promote scanning. Before you determine font size, you're going to want to know more about your typical site visitors. They say that the first thing to go is the eyes (I wouldn't know since my eyesight has been crap since birth. My glasses are so thick that when I look at a map I can see people waving.) If you have customers that are over forty, you will want to keep your website fonts at a comfortable point size. I'd rather they scanned through the text than become annoyed by its small size. I've found that a ten point font (point size is a measurement for font size) seems to be a very happy medium. It's neither too large nor too small. However, if your website attracts senior citizens, you may want to experiment with an eleven or twelve point font. As long as you don't think it looks ridiculously large, then go for it. Yes, I said, "as long as you." While you may not be a website usability expert, I'm still certain of your common sense. Website usability experts may be well versed in the best practices of design, but nothing beats a little common sense and personal brain power.

Take a cue from the theme song to that classic sitcom "Different Strokes" and remember, "What might be right for you may not be right for some." Don't forget that "best practices" are great, but your opinion matters, too. Use your own judgment and your customers won't visit your site and wonder "What you talking 'bout, Willis!"

Another text related issue that is widely overlooked is color blindness. While very few people are 100% percent color blind, a large percentage of people suffer from a degree of color blindness. A client once mentioned that his partial color blindness makes it impossible to read websites with lightly colored fonts on light backgrounds. Now, this may not be a highly common issue, but how much would it suck to do all the work to attract a potential customer, have all the right information, and lose them to a seemingly trivial design flaw? It would suck a lot! Black text on a white background provides the highest contrast, remains easy to read, and just plain works. Why mess with it?

Since we realize that average users scan through website text, make sure the most important content is located at the top of the page. Anything that you absolutely want someone to read should be visually identifiable; e.g. formatting words in bold or in a text box with a light colored background, etc. This high-lighted text is your call to action. Calls to action remain very important. They attract the eye and create that elusive persuasive momentum we are all trying to achieve. If you overuse calls to action, and highlight too much information, you run the risk of diluting your page's effectiveness.

Text that is located at the top of the page may be the most important part of your site. There is a term called "above the fold", which originated in the news-paper industry. Above the fold is anything found above the scroll line. The scroll line is the invisible line that begins at the lowest visible portion of your screen, and requires you to scroll down to see it. Since we tend to scan through text, we are more apt to read items above the fold, and less likely to interact with items below the fold. This does not make information found below the fold useless. There is no way to absolutely quantify site behavior of your individual visitors. Thus, there is really no downside to having elements below the fold. Even if they do not get viewed as often, the additional content will help with search engine placement.

There are an awful lot of useless generalizations within the industry. Some enjoy saying that "people don't read content on a website." Whether it's less or more, don't pay attention to these kinds of comments. Put the right amount of content on your site. By using common sense as your guide, you'll find the right balance. If you think it's important to say, say it! If it never gets read, it's no less important. Furthermore, if the content follows a strategic pattern, it will help your site to achieve stronger search engine rankings.

Getting back to eye tracking; the top of the web page is the first place a typical visitor will look. Then, they scan down the center and most studies show them moving across to the right. This is about the extent of usefulness for the top and right sides. The right hand side remains in a visitor's peripheral, but is not a primary area of focus. Thus, you really don't want to put any sort of critical information in this area. Most studies actually show that websites with advertisements actually experience more ad clicks when it is placed on the left side of the page.

Printing limitations are another reason not to put important information on the right-hand side. Most websites differ in size and resolution from a piece of paper, and tend to cut off the right side when printed. If you have information that people might like to print, then you'll need to be aware of the unprintable portions on your page. Some will tell you to simply create a print-friendly version of the site. Yes (long sarcastic sigh). You can do that, but remember that it will increase the cost of development. By maintaining the information in the right places, this issue solves itself.

Search engines, such as Google, can illustrate the importance of the right and left-hand information rule. The majority of reports and studies, (including my own), tracking search engine click through results show that more searchers click on the left-side results even more than the paid placements on the right. Nearly three times as many people will click on a search result in the "natural" or "organic" search engine results (which are on the left side of Google's website after a search is performed), as opposed to the PPC (Pay Per Click) paid results that appear on the right. People will typically not click on the right, until they're certain they cannot find it on the left.

Alright, enough about the right hand side. I think you get the point. As for looking up, people seem to have stopped looking up years ago. This makes sense to me. I don't see people looking up in my everyday life. Aside from the tourists I see in Manhattan, people don't walk around looking up. It's not a natural thing to do. People look left to right but not up. Scanning left to right is a natural eye movement. Scanning up and down is not. The web industry name for this is "banner blindness." Search engines and portals tend to put advertisements at the top of the page so we've been conditioned to stop looking up. Personally, I find this happening all the time. After I read the content, I look around for navigation. If it's located at the top of the page, chances are I'll miss it.

This leads me to a long-debated topic regarding website usability. Where should you put the navigation on your website? Some studies say left, while some tend toward the top. At the risk of sounding like a politician, I tend to lean to the left as my recommendation for placing navigation. I like the site navigation to be in line with the content, which is always in the center of the page. By placing it left, there is no way to miss it. Your eyes naturally scan from left to right as opposed to up and down. Now I'm not saying that navigation at the top of page is bad. If you make it visible, then it should work just fine. For example, Amazon probably has the best (and most copied) top navigation on the Internet. Amazon uses very visible and very simple tab style navigation. This navigation works very well for Amazon and many other sites. Just use what works best with your website design and make sure it can't be easily overlooked.

One of the biggest mistakes I see is designers incorporating navigation into imagery at the top of a page. This is too easily lost by the user's eye. For that matter, you should not incorporate any important information into the imagery at the top of a page. Too often I see contact information and calls to action meshed in with a graphical header. This information can easily go unnoticed, so make sure you avoid this mistake.

While on the subject of navigation, there is one thing on which most experts agree. Fly out menus suck! Fly out menus are those hand-eye coordination nightmares, which appear when rolling your mouse over a button. Additional menus will fly out, giving you a list of sub pages under the main button. For example, let's take a website that sells music. You may see a button labeled "Buy Music." When you point to this button a menu flies out with genre choices such as Rock, Alternative, Hip Hop, Country, etc. When you point to Rock, another menu would fly out, giving you even more drilled down choices such as Classic Rock, Southern Rock etc.

These fly out menus will either drop from the top when navigation is located at the top of a website or fly out from to the right for left sided navigation. Sometime they even fly out two or three times and if your pointer is off by a millimeter, they all collapse back in. Then you have to keep your hand steady as your pointer gets ever closer to the part of the menu you have to click on to go to the desired page. If you don't have a steady hand, you'll blow it, so be careful! It's like a friggin' game of Operation without the nerve shattering buzzing noise. Why would you want to create a hand-eye coordination skill test for your visitors? Just let them click on a button and then give them choices once they get to the desired page. If you must use a fly-out menu, then you should always allow your visitors to be able to click on the first level button, from the point of origination.

I realize that fly out menus were designed to help categorize information, but there are simply better ways. For categorization – expandable menus work well. This is typically seen in left hand navigation (another reason I like left hand navigation menus). This is when you click on a link and the entire navigation set moves down to reveal more choices. These additional choices will appear under the button you clicked but, unlike fly outs, they are more "static." This means they do not disappear, or require you to roll over the main button to make them reappear. Remember, they should maintain some visual difference from the main navigation buttons. This will highlight their status as an additional choice for the user.

A good example of expandable navigation can be found at `www.BlueClaws.com`. This is the website for a minor league baseball team in Lakewood, NJ. The BlueClaws are the single A affiliate of the Philadelphia Phillies. Because they use good, clean navigation, their website is able to contain a lot of well-organized information. According to their site statistics, the BlueClaws website handles well over two million visitors a year, and not a single page of their website goes unvisited.

Another best practice is to make sure your website conforms to its own styling. All of your font styles and point sizes must remain consistent. (This excludes headlines and emphasized content.) Consistency is the key to professionalism when it comes to website design. Use the same colors for all of your textual links. Textual links are words that are also links to other pages inside or outside your website. The color that is most typically identifiable as a link is blue. People seem conditioned to identify a word in blue as a link, especially if it is blue and underlined. Obviously your links can be any color you want, but blue should be your first choice. On my website all of my textual links are blue, and when you roll over them they turn green. This is done just to reinforce the fact that the text link is clickable. The changing color of the text and mouse pointer–to-pointing hand transformation makes for a link that cannot be overlooked.

Now, conformity does not end with text and link color. As you go from page to page within your website, the conformity of design should be consistent. You don't want people to get confused and think they are bouncing to different websites. Keep everything uniform. Always have a consistent navigation theme on every page. I'm going to repeat that because, well, it bears repeating. Consistent navigation on every page!

I hate going to a website and clicking on a link only to be taken to a page with zero navigation, forcing me to use my browser's back button if I want to get to the site's navigation. I'm sorry but this is just stupid. It shows a lack of professionalism, and indicates that the developer is a lazy bastard. There is something called the "three click rule." Everything on your site should be three clicks from everything else on your site. Clicking my back button forces me to move back in order to move forward – what a waste of a good click. Consistency insures a good experience. Make sure all of the pages on your website match each other and provide quick access to the rest of your site.

So what have we learned in this chapter?

- Consistency is an absolute must on a website;

- Font sizes should be evaluated based on users. Still, maintain a minimum of nine and a maximum of twelve points;

- It's okay to be blue if you're a hyperlink;

- Fly out menus suck!

This is just a glance at website usability best practices, and there is much more to learn. I recommend reading one of the many books dealing with website usability. Do a search on Amazon for "website usability" and you'll find lots of great material to take your understanding to another level. One of the books that I like on the subject is Seth Godin's "*Big Red Fez.*" I mentioned that I shared the speaker's platform with Seth in 2005, but I've been a big fan of his books for some time. *Big Red Fez* is a quick and easy read and highlights Seth's unique style and insights.

Another great usability book is "*Don't Make Me Think: A Common Sense Approach to Web Usability*" by Steve Krug. I like the title (almost as much as mine) because that is truly what it is about. We all want a site to be so simple to use that you don't have to think about it. The last book I would recommend is "*Homepage Usability: 50 Websites Deconstructed*" by Jakob Nielsen and Marie Tahir.

Neither of these latter two books are a quick read. However, the information they cover is very intriguing and useful for anyone developing a website, or looking to make one better. Shouldn't we always be looking for ways to make our marketing better?

8 | MOMMY, IS DADDY SUCCESSFUL?

Defining success through measurability.

What is the true measure of success? How do you define success? Can you define it in your personal life? Can you define success in your professional life? Most people would define their personal and professional success by using words such as happiness, contentment, financial stability, and accomplishment. But wouldn't it be great if there were a software or service to track personal accomplishments, levels of happiness, financial independence and professional accolades? This software could track trends in life and personal development on a daily, weekly and monthly basis, giving you enough details to easily allow the bar for success to be identified and reached. You could look at your success tracking software and see if you are more successful on Thursdays or Fridays, and where success was mild at best. Even better, you could see what parts of your life were not going well, and make immediate changes to get you back on track. Although it would be great, this type of personal tracking software does not exist in life. We are left to our own methods of personal measurement. Fortunately, this kind of measurement does exist for your website.

One of the best things about the Internet is that everything is measurable. This allows you to track your marketing on a granular level, which was not readily available in the past. In fact, by combining your online and offline efforts into a cohesive strategy, you can simultaneously measure both ends of your marketing plan. My rule remains, "If you can't measure it, you can't manage it."

Companies large and small are integrating a web strategy into all of their offline marketing. Offline marketing should drive people to your website. Why? Because any action on your website is measurable! You can track spikes in visitors, entry pages, the busiest weeks of the year, the busiest days of the week, as well as the busiest times of the day. You can see where people enter your website, and from which page(s) they leave. By typing in my URL or from a search engine, I can tell whether a visitor came from another website. I can even see what keywords people are typing into search engines to find my site.

You can really get very granular with your website measurements and tracking, but how can you track offline marketing using your website tools? That's a great question, but before I answer, let me explain the reason this is important.

Marketing fails. In your business, in my business, in everyone's business there are inevitably going to be marketing efforts that just don't produce a return. (To make yourself feel better about spending the money, you can chalk them up to branding. But, who are we kidding?) As professionals, we realize that marketing sometimes fails, but often succeeds. Sometimes great ideas just fail to live up to expectations. The good news is that it's okay to fail. In fact, I consider failure to be a precondition of success. If you don't try new types of marketing you'll never know what does, or doesn't, work. That said, not knowing whether your plan succeeded or failed is unacceptable. This leads to more money being spent on a failed program, and less on something that really produced. You have to build measurability into all of your marketing.

What do you need to grow your business? Revenue. Where does revenue come from? Customers. How do you get customers? Marketing. When revenue is tight what's the first thing to get cut? Marketing.

Doesn't really make sense, does it? Now, if you knew exactly which marketing program was producing revenue, you could channel your budget toward this plan and increase revenue. You would be able to transition budgets from mediocre marketing programs to better performers. All you need is the data to make an educated decision. This is where integrating your marketing efforts into your website becomes a must.

Before we discuss the combination of measurements, we should probably first talk about your online statistics. In fact, a lot of my potential clients seem to have only the vaguest notion as to how their critical online data is accessed.

First, a warning to you technophobes. Don't blank out on me when I use terms like "web server", "hosting," and "log files." I assure you that I will not talk over your heads and make you feel dumb. I'll keep it real simple, and I'll even type very slowly.

Your website resides on a computer. This computer is called a "server." This is similar to the way your office resides in a building. They call it a server because it "serves" up information (in this case the pages contained within your website). Activity on a "web server" (a server designed to serve up web pages) is tracked and recorded. Recorded data is stored in what is called a "log file." This is similar to the way a phone company tracks activity, such as duration and destination of your calls. Are you all still with me? Good, because that was the most technical part. I told you I'd keep it simple.

Log file data allows your web hosting company (the company that owns and maintains the server your website resides on) to monitor what happens on a server. They can then determine the best ways to maintain a server, and identify any issues that arise.

Log files can also be analyzed to view activity and trends on a website. There are specific programs that analyze this log file data and put it into a usable format for easy viewing. There are many different programs out there that work very well. Two that I have personally used are "Live Stats" by Deep Metrix and "Web Trends." You cannot go wrong with either of these, but there are many choices.

From here forward I am going to refer to the data collected in the log files as "stats", and the programs allowing you to view these stats, as "stats programs." Simple enough, right?

Stats programs are primarily "browser based." This means they require no special viewing software, and can be viewed from within browser programs like Internet Explorer, Netscape, Safari, AOL, and Firefox. In essence they are websites that track websites. These stats programs allow you to access information about your website, just as you would access information on any other website. They have links and navigation to access content.

A stats program worth anything should at a minimum allow you to view the following.

- Total number of visitors. Visitors are different than hits. A single visitor can create multiple hits. Every time a picture loads on your site that's a hit. Everything a visitor clicks on is a hit so you want to look at visitors, not hits. A visitor is counted once. FYI: Some stats programs use the word "sessions" as opposed to "visitors." Same thing.

- Date ranges. You should be able to view stats for the day, week, or month.

- Most popular pages. You can see which pages on your website are least and most viewed.

- Entry pages. Not every visitor to your website will enter your site from your home page. Some visitors will go directly to specific pages within your website. This measurement will let you know which pages of your site are showing up in search engines, and will also be important in measuring offline marketing.

- Exit page. Shows where a visitor exits. Exit pages are among my favorite things to measure because they let me know which pages of my site need stronger calls to action, or better messaging. If a lot of visitors are exiting from my "about us" page, then I know that page is not compelling enough to persuade my visitors to stay.

- Referring sites or Referring URL's. This measurement details where visitors come from. You will be able to see which websites sent visitors to your site through links on their page(s). This is also where you would look to see what search engines are sending visitors to your website.

- Key phrases. A good stats program should show you the key phrases and key words visitors used to find your website.

The above items are "must have" measurements for a stats program. Stats programs can and do measure far more than what I've mentioned. These are simply starting points.

So how do you access these stats programs? The company that hosts your website provides you with access to these stats programs. Makes sense – they maintain your web server so they provide access to the log files contained within. Now, if your web host does not provide access to web stats programs or limited access via scheduled reports – fire them! Any halfway decent hosting company that does not provide this basic service should be ashamed of themselves. They are not committed to helping you succeed. Fire them, fire them, *Fire Them*!!!

Now that you know the how's, what's and where's of website measurement, let's take a look at measuring an offline marketing campaign. I have a rule that my marketing team has to adhere to when implementing offline marketing for my company. They can try any kind of marketing program they want…as long as it can be measured. I don't care if a program fails. I care about a program failing and not knowing the reason.

Your website is not static like a printed ad, which means that it can be changed at any time. This gives you a great opportunity to use your website's extreme measurability to measure offline marketing campaigns. All it requires is a little thought.

The simplest way to measure an offline marketing campaign, such as a magazine ad, is to link it into your website. It's sometimes as simple as creating a specific page within your website that ties into a specific offline marketing campaign. You can create a disconnected page within your website (commonly referred to as an orphan page). This disconnected page does not show up in your website's navigation, and stands alone. This disconnected page would have a designated URL to correspond with your marketing program. Another way to do this is to create a stand alone website to back up your marketing campaign.

Example 1: Using a disconnected page to measure marketing.

I'll use my company for the first example. I do a lot of public speaking and, based on the time of year, my presentation is customized to correspond with any upcoming holidays. We've done specific presentations for Valentine's Day where we gave out New England Confectionary Company's Sweethearts® brand candy "conversation hearts" to all of the attendees. Custom labels were created and put on every box. These labels had a tie into my company's offerings and a special offer for attendees of this specific event. All an attendee had to do to access this special offer was type in the special URL (website address) on the box. We did the same thing for Saint Patrick's Day. We used miniature boxes of General Mills' Lucky Charms® Cereal and again, created a custom label. The label contained a picture of the Lucky Charms mascot "Lucky the Leprechaun™" and read "Wanna get lucky? Visit `SingleThrow.com/Luck`."

We created a disconnected page (`SingleThrow.com/ Luck`) that could not be accessed in any way other than typing in the URL, which was only available to people with these special boxes of Lucky Charms. This page carried the same theme as my presentation, and gave visitors a chance to win an Apple iPod® mobile digital device just by joining our monthly newsletter. Our stats program showed the number of visitors this program attracted. We compare that number with how many signed up for the newsletter, as well as the number of event attendees.

We can use our results to determine whether or not this marketing campaign is worth pursuing. We can identify ways to improve. If we had a lot of visitors to the disconnected page, but few signups, we need more compelling reason to sign up. If we failed to attract people to the disconnected page, I might want to push a little harder from the speaker's platform, or change the message on the marketing material. If all of the above proves to deliver little to no results, it might be time to try a completely different approach.

Example 2: Using a stand alone website to back up a marketing campaign.

Oreck Corporation. Oreck® is a successful vacuum cleaner and appliance manufacturer. Oreck markets their famous eight pound vacuum cleaner through multiple channels including advertisements, websites, search engines, etc. Their infomercials feature the founder, David Oreck. I found myself watching this infomercial one Sunday morning when I just happened to be in the market for a new vacuum cleaner. The infomercial was compelling enough to pique my interest in the Oreck brand, which was not even under consideration prior to my watching. David Oreck was the actual presenter, and did an amazing job promoting the benefits of his product. His enthusiasm was inspiring, and truly made me want to own an Oreck vacuum cleaner. David Oreck combines marketing and sales to create results. He spent half an hour touting all the great features that a great vacuum cleaner should have. He then wrapped up by providing the viewer with very compelling offers, and made it a no brainer to try his "Eight Pound Oreck XL®" vacuum risk free.

Throughout the infomercial, viewers were directed to a website for more information and to make a purchase. The URL was provided on screen and through instruction from Mr. Oreck. This website is BuyOreck. com. This is a stand alone website. It is not the main Oreck corporate website. It was created to correspond with the message provided in the infomercial. Specials, benefits, and products perfectly matched those offered in the infomercial. There was absolutely no disconnection from a messaging perspective. The website gave me more detail, as well as product tours, and a lot more information than could ever be covered in a thirty minute television campaign.

The long and short of it is that I purchased the Oreck vacuum cleaner. The combination one – two punch of the television spot and website were so compelling that it knocked all other brands I was considering right out of the running. I immediately purchased the Eight Pound Oreck XL right from the website.

The benefit of this website tie-in strategy for David Oreck goes far beyond my purchasing his vacuum cleaner. It's obvious that Oreck spends a great deal of money on offline advertising and marketing. It's also obvious that they use the web to measure and improve all their efforts. The stats for the Oreck website can track busiest days of the week and times of day. Using this information, Oreck can determine the most effective times to run their infomercials and won't waste time and money running infomercials during poorly performing periods. That is a *huge* cost savings, and allows them to kick back great specials to their consumers. Thus, effective measurement saves David Oreck money, and likely saves some for his customers as well.

After a little more digging I found that Oreck has many stand alone websites, and likely uses them to measure lots of different offline marketing and advertising campaigns. My hat is off to Oreck for doing such a great job, and to David Oreck, for having the foresight to tie all of this together. He has leveraged the Internet into a genuine customer-generating enterprise.

Oh, and by-the-way…I love the vacuum cleaner. It really sucks!

9

MOMMY, I THINK MY INBOX IS FULL

Using email marketing to attract customers.

Mommy, where do customers come from?" is not the only question I can answer. Here's another one. Does size really matter? When it comes to email marketing, it certainly does.

Email has quickly become the communications method of choice for Internet users. It's fast, it's easy, and it just plain works. Email marketing has also quickly become the chosen method for businesses wishing to reach existing and potential clients. It's highly effective, as well. In fact, email marketing has measurable average click through rates of 5 to 15%. Because paper-based campaigns typically receive only a 1-2% response rate, email marketing has become firmly entrenched as the preferred marketing weapon of choice.

If your business is not using email marketing, then you'll need to make note of some statistics:

- Permission-based email is far and away the favorite method of online communication for consumers. Seventy-five percent of users rated it as their preference, with only 25% choosing postal mail, and *zero* selecting telemarketing.

- Permission-based email simply motivates consumers to purchase. Approximately 78% of online shoppers have made purchases after clicking through an email link.

- Email has latent and cross-channel impact. Consumers are inspired to make immediate online and offline purchases, or to return for future transactions.

- During a recent survey, 54% of small businesses rated email as the best online method for driving visitors and customers to their websites.

- Seventy-five percent of executives say that email was their primary source of business information in 2005.

- Jupiter Communications estimates that while paper-based campaigns receive only a 1-2% average response rate, email campaigns can receive 5-15%.

- Email is something all businesses should embrace, but it is not immune to pitfalls. Doing a poor job with email can have very real and lasting repercussions. Like any other marketing operation, success is dependent on proper planning and execution. Sending an email is easy, but an email campaign demands a proper foundation.

So, you're probably still wondering where "size matters" fits in to all of this. Here you go: Because my business provides clients with email marketing, I maintain a unique perspective. Most of my clients view email and direct marketing as being one and the same. In direct mail, your chances for success are bolstered by the number of mailings made. For an email campaign, this becomes a flawed approach. Because direct mail operations only achieve that 1-2% rate of success, more mailings means more response. It becomes a numbers game. The more mail you send out, the greater your chances of generating response and return on investment.

Email is much different. In actuality, when dealing with email, a smaller list is beneficial. Allow me to elaborate. Because less continues to remain more, even at this stage, it is advantageous to create a smaller, more qualified, email list. Sending email off to irrelevant and unqualified recipients is simply a waste of time. Furthermore, with the creation of spam laws, it is not in your best interests to send out unwanted email. Aside from anything else, it makes a bad impression. There is simply no value to gathering up multitudes of email addresses, and building your campaign around a disinterested audience.

A clean "opt-in" list is worth its weight in gold. When a list of interested candidates is generated, your chances of success skyrocket. Because we encourage the creation of quality email lists, my clients routinely see a 17–20% response rate. This may take a bit more time, but the long-term benefits are well worth the wait. In our system, the client is charged for the size of the list, and not by the number of emails sent. This further clarifies the cost savings associated with the creation of smaller, but more targeted email lists.

So the next time someone asks if size really matters, you can absolutely say, "yes, it surely does."

Did you know that once someone has chosen to "opt-out" it is unlawful to put them back on your email list? I mean **never!**

There is far more to email marketing than just understanding the rules surrounding lists. While I'm going to provide some general information, I strongly suggest picking up a couple of the many excellent books written about email marketing.

While I've listed some pretty compelling statistics, I'm certain that some might still be hesitant to use email as a marketing vehicle. Many still think email marketing is intrusive, annoying, daunting and confusing. I have three words for you: **_get over it._** An estimated 60 billion emails are sent daily by Internet users. With this number continually growing, if you don't start to embrace this great marketing tool, your business may not live to regret it.

I'm going to provide some basics of email marketing to help present a clear picture of its power. Email marketing is not something to fear; it is a potent medium with the ability to help generate real and lasting growth for your business.

The Do's and Don'ts of Email Marketing

Don't try to email the masses using the email program on your computer. Email programs such as Outlook, Outlook Express, and Eudora were not designed for mass email. Sure, they can send a message to multiple people, but they just don't have the necessary tools and horsepower associated with effective marketing within this medium.

Desktop email programs do not provide the tracking mechanisms needed to properly manage the process. And, do remember that if you can't measure it, you can't manage it.

In addition, most service providers only allow 50 emails to be sent at one time. Furthermore, sending mass email using these programs does not meet with spam law requirements, and displays a lack of professionalism. Due to the strict and unforgiving spam filters in place today, most email sent using these systems will never even reach their destination. Spam has become such an overwhelming problem that even approved messages occasionally get caught in the filters. Consequently, an unprofessional attempt has no chance!

Lastly, most people using these programs for mass email don't do it correctly. They put all the email addresses in the "To:" field, which lets every recipient see everyone else's email address. Even worse, you run the risk of unscrupulous types adding these people to their lists, which leads me to my second "don't."

Don't add people to your list that didn't ask to be on your list. There is a term called "opt-in." Someone making the choice to be on your list has "opted-in." This means they find usefulness in your information, and have given you their permission to market to them. This is an exceptionally valuable position, so try not to blow it! And now...my final "don't."

Don't be annoying. You should never abuse the privilege of anyone's opt-in status. The average Internet user gets close to a hundred emails a day. If they've shown faith in your company by joining your list, you must respect their time and permission. Send email when you have something worth sending, and never abuse the right, or you're not likely to have it very long.

Okay...let's do some "do's."

Do segment your list. When using a proper email marketing program, the list can be segmented to provide the most relevant information to the most appropriate recipients. Doing this instantly increases the overall results of any email campaign. For instance, Harley-Davidson Motor Company is a Single Throw client, and we handle their email marketing. They segment their list in a few different ways. For example, "Do you own a Harley-Davidson Motorcycle? If you do, which model do you own?" Now you can be emailed when information related to your motorcycle, such as specials on parts, becomes available. If you don't ride (what Harley-Davidson considers an "enthusiast"), you may not receive emails about upcoming group rides. By properly filtering the data, you can create a system providing only useful and relevant information to interested members on your list. In doing so, you'll create a targeted, valuable email strategy which produces content that your customers anticipate and look forward to receiving.

Do use a catchy subject line. However, make certain the information contained within the email is relevant to the title. Being deceptive doesn't work.

Do have an email plan. This may be the most important aspect of email marketing. You wouldn't build a birdhouse without a plan, so don't market your company without one. If you are one of the lucky opt-in recipients of Single Throw's email newsletter, "Traffic Matters," you know that it comes out once a month, and always on a Wednesday after 1:00 PM. Why Wednesday at 1:00 PM you ask? Because we have a plan.

Research has indicated that Mondays and Fridays are bad days to send out marketing material, as people are adjusting to either the beginning or end of their week. Mornings are bad for email as most people are bombarded with it first thing, and end-of-the-day emails get little attention from the tired masses. So, after testing multiple timeslots on Tuesdays and Thursdays, we determined that the largest percentage of people opened and read our emails at 1:00 PM on a Wednesday. Now, had we not created a plan and implemented a professional email marketing program, we would not have been able to maximize the effectiveness of our objectives.

I cannot overemphasize the importance of constructing proper emails. You are sending out official communication from your company for the world to see. Sending out a poorly developed email conveys the same message as delivering a poorly developed product. If the content can't be loaded, or the message can't be opened, it reflects badly on your company. Make certain your email recipients see you at your best.

Each email leaves the recipient with an impression of your company. Should your email be riddled with typos, marked as "junk" or "spam," or use ridiculous colors and fonts, what sort of effect will it have on your customer?

There are many aspects to successful email marketing programs that go far beyond this discussion. Still, when done right, this remains an important and powerful marketing vehicle for your business. Do it, and do it right...or you might end up sending a "going out of business" email someday.

10 MOMMY, CAN I CROSS THE STREET?

Mommy, can I cross the street? Look both ways or the 'traffic' will kill you!

Successful marketing on the Internet is about acquiring good customers. The web allows you a unique opportunity to attract qualified potential customers at their exact moment of need. Throughout this book I've referred to these people as "*imminent buyers.*" They are qualified as *imminent buyers* because they have what is called "purchase intent." Otherwise, they'd not be searching for your products and services.

No matter our chosen marketing strategy, we all want to get in front of well-qualified leads. No businessperson wants to spend time with a disinterested individual. While this obviously sounds logical, most companies still seem to measure the success of their website by the number of visitors, and pay little attention to the quality of their leads.

As I continuously mention throughout this book, a lead that comes from the Internet is usually well-qualified. A searcher starts out with purchase intent. They typically go to their favorite search engine, and seek out their desired product or service. They sift through the bombardment of website listings, and choose to visit your site. Now, if you've done your job correctly, the interest of this potential customer will have been piqued, and they will proceed to make contact. If they've gone to the trouble of making contact, it's fairly likely they're a qualified lead. Keeping in mind that a web visit is a sale more easily lost than made, it remains imperative to do everything right. That's the way to make web sales.

This is how it should be, yet companies still seem to be totally obsessed with blindly increasing the "traffic" to their sites.

Being born and raised in New Jersey, there is one fundamental truth I understand all too well: there is no such thing as good "traffic." Traffic is synonymous with slow downs, accidents and missed opportunities. When did these become good things?

You may have been led to believe that traffic on your website is a good thing. Unfortunately, in most cases, nothing could be further from the truth. Be very wary of the slew of firms promising increased "traffic" to your website. The bare truth is that you don't want random traffic on your website – you want customers. Quantity without quality does not create opportunity.

Perhaps you've been inundated with offers from the many firms offering more traffic at bargain prices. Why not give it a try? Before you do, consider this question: Would you rent a billboard at a tenth of the standard price? You might instinctively be saying yes. However, wouldn't you first want to know where the billboard is going to be located? Now, imagine you were told that it would be placed at the end of a road not traveled, or one packed with completely mismatched, disinterested consumers? For instance, if your product was geared toward women, you wouldn't want the billboard on a road lined with gentlemen's clubs. You'd end up missing your target by marketing on a street traveled by men looking for the local juice bar. You're not likely going to sign that contract. You see how the excitement of the "bargain" fades as the reality materializes? No matter how attractive the price of the bargain billboard appears, its poor placement makes it a poor investment, and simply won't help drive new business.

I once posted a *Wall Street Journal* article that dealt with Internet marketing on my website. It detailed the woes of a leather clothing company. This particular company was banned from Google for using unethical tactics to achieve placement in search engines. (Yes... this really happens!) The article happened to mention the types of leather garments sold by this online retailer. The next thing I know, people typing "leather mini-skirt" into Google are showing up on my website! Boy! Did my traffic increase in a hurry! It seems there are a lot of people out there searching for leather mini-skirts. My site tracked over 3,000 more visitors a week. In a matter of weeks I measured my site traffic to be over 12,000 additional visitors for the month, which was directly attributable to those same leather mini-skirts. And, how much revenue for my company did that generate? None! All that additional traffic didn't add up to one additional inquiry for the types of services I provide. However, I did have a momentary urge to start selling leather mini-skirts.

Here's the point. Even though I was able to measure a significant increase in traffic, I was not able to convert any of these 12,000 visitors into a customer. We were simply irrelevant to each other. Perhaps, you're thinking, "no harm done and you got some more traffic." Not true. What if the visitors confused this article as a "call to action", and I started getting calls and emails about leather mini-skirts? What if the additional traffic slowed my site down or caused it to crash due to the additional drain on server resources? The possibility would exist for me to have lost a great customer because they could not access my site. In a case like this, traffic could cost me dearly. The additional calls and emails also take time to answer, which is a drain of valuable internal resources.

Acquiring and retaining customers on the Internet is a complex process, and requires a thorough understanding of the entire process. This includes sales, marketing, user behavior, and technology. In order to get a return on your marketing dollar, you cannot simply purchase random traffic and hope for a winner. This kind of investment has little chance of generating income.

One of my customers recently shared a story about generating traffic. They implemented an expensive, extensive traffic-building campaign. The solitary goal of this program was to drive as much traffic to the site as possible. There was no strategy to attract specifically interested consumers.

You're probably asking the same question I did – why? They are not in a business that benefits from massive random traffic. So, why make the effort? Have you ever heard the term "smoke and mirrors"? They needed to create the illusion of a busy site in order to get a second round of funding from their investors. Without the prospect of creating sales, it's hard to get funding. For some odd reason, investors always seem interested in gaining a return on their investments. Well, you know what this spike in traffic did for their investors? They wanted to know why the company was failing to convert all that site traffic into real sales. They did not get their funding.

As it relates to the Internet, I'm hoping the term "traffic" will soon go the way of other outdated buzzwords, like "Internet Superhighway" and "Stickiness." Take it from a Jersey guy – don't get caught in online or offline traffic. It just slows you down and keeps you from getting to where you want to go.

11

MOMMY, I THINK THEY'RE TALKING ABOUT ME

Word of mouth, without the mouth?

When asking virtually any businessperson how they get business, you'll almost always get the same answer – Word of mouth. The best business referrals have historically come through word of mouth. I'm sure there was one caveman talking to another about the great job done by the guy who painted his cave. In fact, he was so thrilled to have gotten it done for two carcasses, he tipped him three hides.

In today's world, that cave painter would be found at cavepaintingguy.com. He would post his work and the other cave dudes would email his URL to their interested friends. The word would spread and soon our cave painter would have more work than he could handle. His rates would increase, and he would soon own that great isolated studio cave, near the shady side of the tar pit.

Now, he probably thinks that no one shares his cave painting skills, so he never hires anyone. He is soon so busy that he stops returning emails. His quality slips because he is overloaded. Next thing you know, he's receiving complaints on cave decorating forums, which begins to discourage his potential customers. Word spreads across the internet, and our poor cave painter's business fades. Just like that – he's extinct. I've seen it happen a million times! In fact, I challenge you to find me a quality cave painter – can't be done. What do you think happened to them all? A word to the wise, word of mouth works both ways.

There's an old saying, "that if you do a good job for someone, they will tell 2 or 3 people. Do a bad job and they will tell 15 to 20." Each of us has likely had an experience which supports this claim.

Before the Internet, word of mouth was spread from one person to the next during passing conversations, or when asked for advice by an interested friend.

Word of mouth will always remain a viable way to generate leads. So what's changed? Communication has changed. Just as our cave painter's customers emailed each other, so do *connected customers*. You can email more than one person at a time. You can send a comment, picture, or complaint to fifty people with one click on the mouse.

Have you ever heard of forums? Also known as message or bulletin boards, the Internet-savvy had already developed them into a popular means of communicating well before most of us had dialed-up our very first, and painfully slow, Internet connection.

There is a forum for every earthly and super galactic topic. No matter what your hobby, job, or need, you can rest assured that someone is discussing it online, right now. Forums are places where people from all over the world, with similar interests, meet up for discussion. I use two such forums on a regular basis. One of my hobbies is motorcycle riding, and I own a Harley-Davidson. Anyone owning a Harley can attest to the fact that buying upgrades can quickly become an obsession.

The thing is, motorcycle upgrades don't come cheap, and this is where the forum I frequent becomes highly useful. I can go online at any time day or night and post questions about the upgrade I'm considering. I can discuss good and bad experiences with those who have made the same upgrade. This forum has helped me make better decisions about my motor-cycle, which saves me money, time, and continues to increase the enjoyment of my experience. On the flip side, I've also been talked into a couple of upgrades I hadn't considered – which hasn't saved me money.

Another forum I use is for my dog, Holly. Holly is a Jack Russell Terrier, and was purchased on Christmas Eve (hence, the name Holly). Holly was in the pet store for five months, which is way too long for a dog to live in a cage. Once we saw her, it became clear that she needed to come home for Christmas. She's a great dog and I'm glad she is part of my life. Still, I had an issue that I could not seem to resolve on my own. As a point of information, using a crate has become a proven method for housebreaking a dog. The dog remains in a crate when unattended, and I take her out to do her business when I get home. Being pack animals, the theory is that dogs will not soil their crate, which they consider to be their den. However, being in a pet store cage for so long, Holly had no such instinct, and this method wasn't working. In fact it had gotten so bad that it became the norm to refer to Holly's crate as "the monkey cage", but I digress.

After a multitude of books and no salvation, I turned to the Internet. With a simple Yahoo! search for "Jack Russell Forums", I found my solution. Within an hour of posting my issue, those with similar experiences came out in droves. The advice started pouring in. I'm happy to say that Holly is much better. Thanks to that Jack Russell Forum, she is now trained to ring a bell by my back door when she needs to go out. I also got some great advice on stain and odor removers. While that may be on the wrong side of "too much information," I mentioned it to make a point. When people in both the Jack Russell and Harley-Davidson forums have good product experiences, they really enjoy spreading the news.

There are over 3,000 and 6,000 members, respectively, on the Jack Russell and Harley-Davidson forums I've mentioned. If just one forum member has a bad experience with a product or service, they are not going to tell 10 or 20 people – they are going to tell thousands all at once!

Forums are great. They are communities of like-minded people helping each other. They are like virtual support groups. Friendships are formed, people meet, and problems are solved. This is the new word of mouth.

Here are a couple of other examples of the ways in which forums are changing word of mouth, and benefiting businesses smart enough to leverage them.

SuicideGirls.com is a website and forum that has gained national exposure in *Rolling Stone* magazine, as well as in an HBO documentary. It's a forum for the pierced and tattooed lifestyle. I find it to be a really interesting site, but it's not for everyone.

I recently observed a spike in one of my client's website stats and tracked it back to SuicideGirls.com. It seems that a young woman had work done at a local New Jersey salon. She was very satisfied and posted her satisfaction with this particular salon on the forum. Within an hour, 400 people clicked on the link in her post, and visited the website for this salon. Because her message was positive, I have to believe the salon received a flurry of new business. A simple comment on an obscure message board might have generated a substantial revenue increase for this salon. What if the post had been negative? This salon would have suffered adverse effects and lost potential customers forever.

This is the power of the post –the new word of mouth maintains awesome power and reach and is changing businesses with the click of a mouse. The "network that no one owns" has given power to the people – and they use it. It can work wonders for those who deliver on their promises, and cause misery for those who don't.

How can you leverage the power of the post for your business? One of our clients is in the assisted living business. They have locations in New Jersey, Florida, Virginia and Ohio.

Having learned a good deal about this industry, it's clear that placing one's parents in an assisted living facility is often harder on the adult child than the parent. My client runs offline support groups to help adult children cope with many of the feelings associated with this experience.

My client is now creating an online forum to help adult children deal with their issues. Now people in similar situations can meet online, and help each other through the process.

This forum is a tremendous tool. Those involved can discuss any number of topics. They will meet others in the same situation. They can get support and advice. They can discuss facilities and get feedback on the quality of their services. My client has created a wonderful device for both his industry and community.

Now let's look at this from a business perspective. People shopping for assisted living facilities are already stressed out. Because they are dealing with such a sensitive and personal issue, they are likely to be resistant to a heavy-duty sales onslaught. Many people tend to distrust salespeople, a group likely to include those in this situation. In the absence of trust, those selling assisted living services will have a more difficult time getting these customers to discuss their true needs and issues.

By monitoring posts made in the forum, my client can read what people are saying to their peers. They can finally get to the root of the issues and needs of their potential clients and make appropriate modifications in their services. They can also see what people are saying about their service. They can make the good things better and address deficiencies more rapidly. They can also gather more data about their competitors and use it to enhance their market position.

Whether or not it's a forum you've created, corporate, customer and competitive intelligence can still be easily extracted. Anyone can find, join, and contribute to any forum. While participation might require membership or registration, there is rarely a fee involved. You will then have an opportunity to hear what real people are saying about your industry, clients, and services. You can easily use this information to create a competitive advantage, while bettering your customer connections, and offering more well-designed products and services. In this case, my client will be able to ease their customers through a rough time, by providing greater comfort in their decision.

This is the power of the post. This is the new word of mouth. This is the way in which *connected customers* are communicating. This is what happens when you take the mouth out of "word of mouth."

12

MOMMY, WHERE DO BABIES COME FROM?

How things work

I was one of those annoying little kids who was totally enthralled by the way things worked. I spent a great deal of my childhood taking things apart just to try and figure out how they did what they did. I spent an equal amount of time blowing things up and setting my army men on fire but that's a story for another book. I must have driven my parents nuts because I was truly adept at taking things apart, but really didn't develop the skills to put them back together until later in life.

When I first started in the Internet business, I knew nothing about Internet technology. My obsessive personality fed my thirst for knowledge. I needed to know how the Internet worked. Once I acquired this knowledge I became intrigued with search engines and how they did what they did. At that time there were only a few search engines. Yahoo! was the biggest, but more a directory than a true search engine. A directory categorizes websites by specific pre-set categories, places them in alphabetical order...not unlike the Yellow Pages. AltaVista was a very popular search engine in those days. I remember reading that AltaVista was the search engine of choice for librarians. Given that Internet technology was well on its way toward making libraries obsolete, I was rather struck by that information.

As new search engines began popping up, I was really able to dig into the inner workings of their website ranking methods, and use it to help my clients gain a distinct market advantage. Back then, you really didn't have companies strictly focused on search engine placement and Internet marketing. It was still a website developer's task to make sure you had the keywords in place to attract search engine listings.

Even back then I realized the important role search engines would play in attracting potential customers. (I was a friggin' visionary.) While my company primarily designed websites, we did not classify ourselves as a website development company. Our tag line was "Internet Advertising" because that was my view of the web. It was a great way for companies to advertise to those online. Because search engines were being used to seek out the details of each site, it became clear that this should be the vehicle of choice for promoting web offerings. Visionary...remember?

Today close to 80% of Internet users find their desired products and services by using a search engine. It is critical to understand both the importance and fundamental operating patterns of search engines. Search engines are far more complex than they were in 1995, when I started my first company. As of this writing, there are roughly 600 billion web pages on the Internet. Google is the world's largest search engine, and has about 18 billion pages within its indices. The sheer number of websites has forced search engine companies to modify their methods of determining relevancy.

As the Internet continues to evolve, new technologies and websites are regularly introduced. Search engines evolve at a similar pace, changing the rules in their never-ending efforts to provide searchers with the best results possible. Let's face it, search engines are free tools, and there are many from which to choose. Our loyalty to these search engines is fleeting. As soon as a search engine lets us down and does not show us the most relevant results, we go elsewhere. This is the driving force behind the constant evolution of relevancy rules.

I don't expect the average person to spend as much time as I did in a quest for understanding, so I'm going to help you appreciate these rules and the manner in which they are changing. Still, please do not expect this to be the magic catalyst that instantaneously launches your relevancy into perfect orbit. Search engines are very complex, and their rules are ever-changing. You should still look into hiring a professional firm to help you achieve and maintain the kind of strong placement that grows along with your company. By developing this understanding, you'll be able to make a good choice when selecting an Internet marketing provider.

Let's examine some of the more important aspects of search and try to debunk some of the myths surrounding marketing in the world of search.

As I've mentioned, there are thousands of search engines on the Internet, and the major search engines account for roughly 98% of all search traffic.

The major search engines display results in two primary formats:

- Organic (also called natural or relevant) search results;

- PPC listings (Pay Per Click) are often listed as "sponsored links."

Organic results are listings generated by genuine relevancy to a given search. PPC results are paid for by the advertiser every time someone clicks on the listing.

Let's look first at the organic listing. Organic search listings provide the best return on investment, but remain the hardest to generate.

Organic listings take up the most space on the search results page – typically right down the center of the page, where most searchers look. You cannot pay for these results. Organic (or relevant) listings are there because they are germane to the current user's search phrase or keyword.

These organic search results are highly sought after by businesses. According to a recent Jupiter poll, organic listings account for 85% of commercial referrals from a search engine. According to a recent survey, those clicking on organic listings are more likely to buy than those attracted through Pay Per Click. Thus, it's no wonder that organic placement is so desirable.

In a perfect world, the top listings would absolutely be the most relevant. Given the absence of this perfect world, it remains possible to manipulate and trick the technology to undermine the rankings process. Those engaging in this process are often able to get irrelevant sites placed in highly sought-after positions. It is called "search engine spamming," and remains a battle for search engine companies.

One example of spamming involves placing white text against a white background, making it invisible to the user. However, a search engine spider would pick it up. Another form is something called "cloaking," in which a devious programmer uses technology to determine whether a search engine spider or an actual visitor is viewing the site. The visitor sees the actual website, but the spider sees a page overstuffed with repetitive phrases and keywords.

Search engines frown upon all these methods, and for those caught spamming, it may result in a complete banning or blacklisting from the search engine. When one considers that Google currently garners over 40% of all search traffic, getting banned can cost a company dearly. If a search engine can see it, but a visitor can't, the rule of thumb calls it spam. Avoid companies using such tactics to gain ranking.

There is no easy way to show up in the organic results of a search engine, and those saying otherwise are dirty stinkin' liars. Everything needs to be done the hard way. Fortunately, the hard way is the right way and will always produce the best results.

Another common claim maintains that background "META tags" and "keywords" are all a site needs to show up in search engines. META is one of those rare words in technology that is not an acronym. META does not stand for anything. It's short for *metalinguistics*, which basically means information about information. META keywords in the background code of your website are supposed to dictate your position to the search engines. Not going to happen. Years ago, META keywords helped determine relevancy, but they began to become a source of abuse. People started adding their competitors' names to their META keywords, while using words like "sex" <u>and</u> "dog", which are highly used in searches. (Please notice that I underlined "and" to avoid any confusion.)

About two years ago search engines began to develop better ways to determine relevancy. Search engines created a standard that I call "social rules." For example, we've all heard our mothers say, *"don't say anything if you have nothing nice to say!"* Well, same goes for your website. Search engines only want websites with meaningful and useful content. If you have something good to say, search engines will have an interest in listing your website.

You are judged by the company you keep. This is another social rule adopted by search engines in their quest to rank the best websites. Search engines look beyond the walls of your website to determine relevancy. They look at your links, and at those linking to your site. They follow links from other sites to yours (a great way to attract search engine spiders), so that both sites benefit from any existing relevancy. Conversely, they also follow links from your site to other sites. They want to see any other information a visitor can access by visiting your website. The caveat here is, you have to link to sites that are relevant to yours. What kinds of links might be beneficial to your visitors? Does another site provide a related product? Find a link and add it to your site. This creates value for your visitors and inspires search engine placement.

There are other more "tech forward" techniques used by search engines as well. Before we review some of those, please remember that before you can be organically listed with a search engine, you'll need to make them aware of your existence. If your website shows up in search engines now, you're already ahead of the game...even if it shows up with poor placement. Unlisted websites will take much longer to get indexed than those already in the system.

Search engines use programs called "spiders" (also referred to as Robots, Bots, Web Crawlers and Crawlers) to gather data on a website. Attracting these spiders to your site is the first step to getting indexed. There are many ways to invite these spiders. One way is to use the registration pages provided by most search engines. After registration, your site is presumably placed on a list, which is used by the spider to find your website.

I used the word "presumably" in the last sentence for a reason. Registration is not always effective in getting spiders to your website. It may be that a lot of the search engines ignore these inclusion requests and have the registration process in place as a formality. The search engines might simply be inundated with requests and slower to react. Google's form is located at `www.google.com/addurl/?continue=/addurl`.

The first sentence above the registration form reads as follows:

> We add and update new sites to our index each time we crawl the web, and we invite you to submit your URL here. We do not add all submitted URLs to our index, and we cannot make any predictions or guarantees about when or if they will appear.

Thus, I still feel that websites should be registered on a regular basis. This is a living process, and needs regular attention and should be part of a maintenance program. This also must be done by hand. There are lots of companies out there charging nice fees to register you with thousands of search engines. These companies typically use software to do this. The major search engines do not allow software submission.

AltaVista was the first search engine to start blocking software submissions by integrating a visual word recognition feature into their registration process. When you visit Google's registration page the same word verification exists to block automated submissions. Like I said earlier, there is no easy way to do this and that is by design. Search engines do not make it easy. They want you to work for it, because they know the value of a favorable organic listing. They figure that if you're willing to work for it, you might have a site worth seeing.

A bit more about spiders. Spiders are specifically designed to gather information. There is nothing complex about a search engine spider. I am fond of saying that they are very dumb programs designed by very smart people. All these spiders do is go from one web page to another, gathering up content contained within your website, as well as in the background code (META data – I'll explain later). This is why I harp on the fact that content is very important when it comes to your site design. Search engine spiders are blind. They cannot see images contained within your website, nor can they see any text within the image. Here's a rule of thumb: if you can cut and paste the text, a search engine can read it. You cannot cut and paste images or content created using flash.

Spiders gather the content on your site for analysis by the search engine. However, a spider visit to your website does not automatically mean inclusion in the index. The collected data now goes through a detailed filtering process to determine your relevancy and related keywords.

Major search engines use mathematical formulas called *algorithms* to determine your level of relevancy. We can provide a basic understanding of algorithms by breaking down their description. There are four basic components within these algorithms; prominence, proximity, density and frequency. All the major search engine algorithms apply these principles to their systems. However, each search engine assigns a different standard of importance to each component. This is called "weighting." Each search engine has a slightly different weighting to components within their algorithms. This is why you get different results for the same search phrase in Google, Yahoo!, ASK and MSN. No one knows for sure (other than the search engines themselves) exactly what weighting each search engine uses. They each have their own "secret sauce," if you will.

The first component is **Prominence**. Search engines determine prominence in much the same way you and I would. They search a website for things that stand apart, such as bolded phrases, links to more information, and key terms found "above the fold" (top of a website before the scroll line). Remember, those first words a visitor sees are of great interest to the search engines. Words at the top of your website have more prominence than those at the bottom. Your home page has a higher prominence value than any other page within your website because it's *first*.

When writing website content, you can forgo the "welcome to our website", "feel free to browse our site" or "thanks for stopping by" sentiments. There's really no need to say thanks or welcome a person to your site. In fact, I am free to browse your website, with or without your permission. I don't need you to tell me any of those things. These types of touchy-feely statements are a waste of words and valuable prominence. All they do is slow the process of people getting to the right information. They push relevant information further down the page. If you truly want me to have a great experience on your website, make it easy for me by giving me quick access to information.

There are other components within your website that can lead to better prominence. You can create links within content to take a visitor to other areas of your website. For example, on my website you can hire me as a speaker, or find a list of my speaking engagements. We use sentences such as "find public speakers in NJ" as a call to action. The operative link in this sentence is actually *public speakers in NJ*, which takes you to the public speaking portion of our site. We could have used the term *click here* as the link, but that would only serve to increase the prominence of the term *click here*. The critical search phrase *public speakers in NJ* would be null and void. Are you getting it? Prominence is anything that stands out above everything else.

Proximity is the next component. Proximity is determined by the relation of a phrase or keyword to itself. For example, if the term "Single Throw" is used in a sentence, how many characters or words are there until it is used again? With some creative copywriting you can always find ways to end a sentence, and start the next one, with the same relevant phrase. The only characters between the two would be a space and a period.

Creative copywriting does not mean word stuffing. Your content needs to be well-written and meaningful. If you write strictly to show up in a search engine, you will miss the mark in connecting with your potential customers. Favorable search engine placement is only one piece of the puzzle. You can have great placement and still not achieve success. Your content must be a good mix of quality information and *persuasive momentum*. Although this is not easy and requires talent and thought, a good copywriter understands the ways in which people interact with content on a website. You'll need to achieve a strong balance between being a website that converts visitors into customers, while showing up in front of those potential customers in search engines.

Density. Density is strictly a mathematical formula, and easy to understand. A search engine will take a look at all of the words used on your site and assign each word a percentage value. Does the term "Single Throw" represent 1%, 4%, or 10% of my website's content? Actually, it represents 6.45% of the content on my home page. While that is a high percentage of density for a phrase, it is the name of my company and will be used throughout our site. The density of the phrase "Single Throw" is good, but I don't need to optimize my content in order to show up under my name. If someone is typing my name into a search engine, they already know about my company, quite possibly through some other type of marketing program.

Increasing the density to my name would be a flawed strategy. I should always show up under my name as long as my website is search engine friendly. An uncommon company name maintains a better chance of showing up. My company name is a common term in electronics, but we have a much better Internet marketing strategy than all those other bozos.

Some of the phrases that produce the most qualified leads for my website are "Internet marketing consultants" and "customer acquisition." The phrase "Internet marketing consultants" has a density percentage on my home page of 3.56% and "Customer Acquisition" comes in at 3.05 percent. Either of these phrases typically put us on page one of any major search engine. Still, remember what I said about balance. Your site can achieve too much density. An unusually high density to a specific phrase may be interpreted by a search engine as possible spamming.

Finally, there is **Frequency**. Frequency is simply a word count. How often is each word or phrase used throughout the content of a website? Again, keep it simple. Unusually high frequency levels for specific phrases will cause red flags alerting the search engines to possible "keyword stuffing." Keyword stuffing is simply the overuse of a phrase for the sole purpose of showing up in a search engine.

Keep in mind that a search engine can interpret misuse of these components as an attempt to spam. Always try to remember the goal of your website, and develop the information to guide your visitor. Don't simply develop the content of your site to achieve a strong search engine ranking, or you'll risk alienating a potential customer. Useful information that gives visitors what they came for will provide a true return.

Follow these rules, and you will develop a visitor friendly site that will help you attract and convert potential customers. Develop a website that your visitors find valuable, and the search engines will follow.

Pay Per Click (PPC) or Keyword Bidding

Most major search engines have PPC listings. They are typically on the right hand side of the page and clearly marked "Sponsored," or "Paid," or some variation on the theme. For smaller businesses, PPC has become a do-it-yourself solution. Google actually promotes its "AdWords" program, stating that you can be up and running in as little as 15 minutes.

PPC programs are great for targeting very "aggressive" phrases. These are phrases that return a large number of results in the organic listings. The more sites that show up in a given search, the more difficult it is to make a good showing. For instance, a phrase such as "Real Estate" is extremely aggressive (returning over 832 million pages in Google's results alone). This phrase is also fairly ambiguous. Most local agencies would be better served by creating a strategy to show up under a regional or local search term in the organic listings, such as "Real Estate Toms River NJ." However, a national agency, with offices all over the country, might opt to create a PPC campaign for the generic term. Then, as searchers click through to their sites, give them the choices to localize from there.

Another great use of PPC would be for terminology that changes regularly such as model numbers or product names. When you have products that change model numbers, you might opt to create a PPC campaign.

Before venturing into the world of PPC:

1. You are paying every time someone clicks on your listing. This can get quite expensive, especially if you pick the wrong phrases and do not convert visitors into buyers. Make sure you set budgets and realistic limits. Be aware that you can also get into a bidding war with a competitor, as the highest bidder typically shows up first. And, don't click on your competitor's link to drive up his cost. This is a real concern. Google recently settled a 90 million dollar lawsuit for not putting safeguards in place to prevent "click fraud." My guess is that this problem will soon be rectified.

2. You must still choose relevant phrases or words. Google's "AdWords" program has a relevancy factor built into its system, so top positioning does not always go to the top bidder. Google's PPC listings feature a little green bar titled "interest," which measures the interest level or amount of clicks your listing gets. The interest level and bid rate will determine the placement of your ad. If you generate no interest (or clicks) by picking the wrong phrase, you risk being banned from purchasing those particular words. Google also measures back clicks to determine how many people go to your site from your ad and then hit the back button to return to the search listings. To Google, this means they had no interest in what you had to offer.

Picking the right phrases is paramount for success. Keywords are not good targets anymore. The web has become too vast. You need to get very specific when determining what to target. Remember the three-to-five word phrases being used in the average Google search? MSN statistics say that over 50% of searches go unanswered. Think about what that means…it means that most businesses are choosing the wrong phrases to target and missing a connection with potential customers. You must make sure you choose your phrases wisely.

To create a successful PPC program, keep some of our rules in mind. Use titles and descriptions that have persuasive momentum. Don't drop a visitor on your home page when they click on your paid link. Create a stand alone (orphan) page, so you can leverage the existing train of thought and measure which phrases are working for you. And, I've already harped enough on measurability.

If your PPC budget is exceeding $1,000 per month, it may be time for you to consult with a company that specializes in maximizing the effectiveness of PPC campaigns. They will have the tools and necessary experience to monitor, measure and be proactive when needed. As always, there are both good and bad companies servicing this area. I'll give you an example.

I have a client named Branches Catering (www. BranchesCatering.com), in West Long Branch, New Jersey. Branches is a top notch facility, and we use them for many of our own events. Before becoming a client, their PPC program was being handled by another firm. When I investigated the results of their program, I found some disturbing information. The program was slapped together with very little thought. In fact, Branches was actually paying for their name, meaning one of the phrases this company targeted was "Branches Catering." With some minor website optimization, Branches Catering would already have shown up under their name, and they did not need to waste money buying the phrase. Today, when you search for "Branches Catering", they are actually number one in Google's organic results.

They were also showing up under "Catering Facility NJ." This would have been terrific, if their description didn't read "Wedding Reception Hall NJ." Their old vendor used the same ad and text for all their targeted key phrases. This caused a big disconnection and loss of opportunity. All of the ads brought everyone to the Branches homepage. Given that the site was not (at the time) very easy to use, it was likely discouraging visitors to go right to a competitor's page. Bringing PPC visitors directly to the Branches home page also led to a loss of campaign measurability. Branches could not quantify any working elements of the campaign, which turned out to be very little.

BranchesCatering.com has now been completely overhauled and their leads have increased a thousand fold. They are attracting and converting visitors into customers and have a website that supports their gorgeous facility, incredible food and impeccable service. Once people were able to find them, Branches made them very happy. If you type "Catering Facility in NJ" into Google, they are typically right on page one, where they should be. (Go ahead and try it…I know you want to!)

I'm not expecting that you should now be able to do this for yourself. The web is growing and search engines are in constant change. If you are to keep up, you'll need to hire a professional. Still, I hope you now maintain a greater knowledge of how things work, and the amount of effort required to do this properly. This will help justify the investment, and prevent your being taken in by firms making over-the-top promises. Your best defense against being taken is to be better educated. I hope this chapter helped.

13

MOMMY, I'M STUCK

Tips to make the right choices the first time

I t's quite rare for me to come across a website that I can't make better. A website can always be better, and that mean easier to use. So, when you think you've got it perfect, go back and make it even better.

Certain design elements, technologies, and programming methods not only make a website harder to use, but invisible to search engines. More often than not I find myself fixing elements on my clients' websites that never should have been there in the first place. I'm quite often the bearer of bad news – "I know you paid a lot of money to have this done but it has to be changed because it's preventing you from achieving success." Those search engine spiders can actually be confused by the technology someone used to make you look cool. When it comes to search engine placement this spells trouble. Remember, search engine spiders are dumb programs written by smart people. Rule of thumb – keep it simple.

I'm assuming that a majority of you reading this book are reexamining your website, in the process of redeveloping a website, or creating one from scratch. For you, this chapter will help avoid the creation of barriers to entry. To those who have already created these barriers – sorry, this might hurt a little.

Programmers ▪ Living, breathing barriers.

In most cases, a website is a marketing solution, and not a technological solution. Technology is simply the medium used to transmit the message. While a printer is skilled at operating printing equipment, it's unlikely that you'll want him to design your magazine ad. The same thought process applies to the web. Just because someone can program a website does not mean they should design it. Once it's been researched, planned, and written by a qualified marketing team, the programmer can be used to engineer the site.

I have a specific mindset when it comes to my view of technical people, specifically programmers. Programmers (some, not all) tend to work in little cubes and be slightly introverted (no social graces). They have very narrow views of the world and rarely leave their comfort zone. You cannot expect them to look at things from your perspective. I've worked with a lot of programmers in my career and 8 out of 10 seem to fit this mold. I've become accustomed to referring to them as "pack wolves" because someone told me "idiots" was too harsh.

You can typically see the wolves interacting with their pack outside of your office window as they stand in a circle in front of the office, smoking cigarettes, and discussing how everyone else but them is wrong about everything. Heaven help the lone wolf programmer trying to infiltrate the pack. He or she will be greeted with snarls and furled eyebrows, and their skills as a programmer will be systematically ridiculed as soon as they leave. There are very few standards when it comes to programming, and each programmer believes their kung fu to be better than everyone else's kung fu. This is the stuff that can get *you* into trouble.

A skilled programmer can, and will, program anything you want, but rarely maintains the insight to design what you need. They're not typically good at customer service, and do not want to hear from you once the project is finished. All these factors can lead to an over usage of technology, and again, can get you in trouble.

Now, I may have a narrow view when it comes to programmers, and I could be exaggerating to make my point. One thing I'm not overstating is the negative effects generated by the overuse of technology, which can hurt your website's chances of achieving success.

Now, here is where I come to the defense of our friend the programmer, and pick on you. If you allow your site to be developed without having a clear understanding of the plan and implementation technology, then any arising issues are your fault.

Programmers just do what they do best – program. You may say, "I just don't understand what they are talking about." **Stop Whining!** You need to suck it up and work to understand what they are talking about, because it's your tush on the line. You're the customer. If you don't understand, make them explain it until you do. It's your job as the client to maintain a working understanding of the process. It's their job to help you understand. If they can't – fire them! Throw a rock out the office window and you'll hit another web developer- hire them! Get it? It's your money. You need to understand what is going on or you can count on spending more money down the road.

Technological Barriers

Technology for the sake of technology helps no one.

When it comes to using technology on your website you need to be aware of what, why, and where it's being applied. Additionally, you need to be mindful of a few basic technologies that are often used. When properly implemented, these systems can be of great benefit. Used poorly, they become an impediment to success.

Sessions ▪ To track or not to track?

Sessions is a tracking technology that allows you to track and record a user's activity throughout a website. This is how it works. A unique ID number is assigned to a website visitor when they enter a website. This ID number follows the user throughout every visited page, and right through to a purchase or contact. A website owner can look up reports and see how a specific ID number used the site; for example, ID# 223344W entered the website via the home page on 3/23/2006. They spent 9.2 seconds on the home page and then clicked on the "About Us" page, where they stayed for 4.2 seconds before exiting the website.

You can obviously gather a tremendous amount of user detail from sessions. Still, you need to ask yourself a few questions before implementing it on your website. Do you need this much visitor data and, if so, where is it needed? Where do you really need to track activity? Will you actually even review this data and use it to make the visitor experience better?

You may be asking yourself, "it sounds like sessions are pretty sweet and they gather good information. What is the downside of using sessions?" Great question! Sessions have been called, "the kiss of death," when it comes to search engines. Sessions could make your entire website invisible to search engines – *Great!* You'll be able to tell if visitor number 224433 farts while viewing your website but he might be the last guy to ever find your site. (I just had to get the word fart into this book – makes me chuckle every time I read it.)

You can tell if a website is using sessions by looking at the address bar in the web browser and see if the URL contains the term "sessionid=." This is followed by numbers, letters, or a combination of both.

For example, if my website used sessions you might see the URL as follows – `http://www.singlethrow.com/about_us/sessionid=OU812?`

Sit back, while I explain why this is bad. That URL only exists for one visitor. It cannot be copied and pasted into an email and sent to someone, because as soon as that visitor leaves, the URL ceases to exist. The session ID "OU812" was assigned to one visitor and one moment in time and will not be used again, making that URL "unique." Search engines cannot list unique pages in their index. Most major search engines require that a site be replicated before it can be indexed. Since sessions add a unique ID number to the URL, they fail this test, and remain unique to each individual visitor.

If you still do not grasp the concept of session IDs, it's fairly safe to say that you have no use for them. You can email me any specific questions you may have at *Larry@LarryBailin.com*. Just remember, session ID's are the kiss of death when it comes to search engines.

Session IDs can be useful but aren't required on every page. You can get a good site measurement on most pages from your website stats program. For most website owners the stats program provides plenty of detail to properly and effectively measure activity on your website. Now, if you have a dynamic application such as a shopping engine, you may want to track activity with more detail. (FYI…dynamic applications pull information from a database in real time.)

Sessions allow you to see when shopping carts are abandoned so you can make the process or product offerings better. You can measure things like the number of visitors making it past step five, in a six-step checkout process. This can help determine whether or not you need a simpler process. You can also see what products are most added to the carts of the users that never reach checkout, and which items are viewed the most, but never get put into a cart. Lots of great information can be gathered using sessions but rarely does a website ever need all pages trackable using sessions. Only use sessions when and where necessary, and only if you are going to actively use the data gathered. If you are not going to use the data then don't bother using sessions.

Alright, enough about sessions – I can't take it anymore! I need a drink!

Frames ▪ If your website has been framed, you will end up taking the fall.

Frames are for pictures not websites. The technique of using frames on a website is old and outdated and not used all that often anymore. Any developer that uses frames to build a website is either lacking in skills or simply a lazy wolf. Sorry, Developers. Get over it – the new millennium has started. Didn't you get the memo?

We've all been to websites where the left hand navigation never moves and the content on the right scrolls up and down. This is framing. The original reason for this was to allow pages to be added to a site without having to install navigation on each one. Only the navigation frame would be modified. In theory this is a good idea. However, there are many pitfalls to using frames, and much better alternatives have made themselves available.

The pitfalls are plentiful when it comes to frame usage on a website. To begin with, they are **not** search engine friendly. There may be frame-developed websites on a search engine, but they will always garner a poor showing. A non-framed site is far more search engine friendly – period.

Let's review. Search engine spiders are dumb programs, and don't realize when a website is in frames. They tend to get trapped in a single frame of the website. They either get trapped in the navigation frame, and can't see the content, or get trapped in the content frame and think there is no navigation. Typically, they end up in the content frame and then deduce only one page to the website exists. This is because the navigation frame is invisible to the spider. Okay…everyone exhale.

Search engines will index single content pages from a website using frames. When this happens and a visitor clicks on the link to go to this framed website they end up seeing just that one content page without the corresponding navigation frame. Then, just like the search engine spider, they think one lone page is the extent of the site. The typical visitor will hit the back button and choose the competitor.

I've even seen websites that use three and four frames. They might use a top frame for the logo or header image, a left frame for navigation, one on the right for content, and a bottom frame for some sort of footer. You end up with scroll bars all over the website. This is terrible. If your site looks like this, you should smack your developer around a little – they deserve it.

Here are some other issues caused by frames. As your visitor goes from page to page of your framed website, the URL never changes. To avoid a painful technical explanation, I'll be brief. The URL is "attached" or "assigned" to one of the frames that does not change (such as a navigation or a top header frame). This means your visitor cannot put a specific page into their favorites or bookmarks. It also means they cannot cut and paste the URL for a specific page to email off to a friend or colleague. Because the interface is unwieldy, a visitor may also have issues printing some pages when frames are used.

The long and short of it is that using frames to program a website is neither good design nor search engine friendly. Other technologies now exist which allow you to maintain your website with the same ease and efficiency associated with frames.

An example of an alternative search, visitor, and maintenance friendly technology is called "includes." The website for this book (`MommyWhereDoCustomersCom eFrom.com`) uses this simple technique. My navigation is an "include" which means that my programmer created the navigation once and told it to "include" itself on every page. You get it? Simple. Right?

I can add a new page or navigation to my site, or link to my existing navigation. And, since my navigation uses "includes," it will essentially replicate itself on every page. This technique is simple, effective, and efficient. Includes are visitor and search engine friendly, and make the task of growing, maintaining and changing your website a lot less labor intensive.

Includes are widely used and have really almost become the standard, at this point. If your website developer has at least half a brain, they should be able to use this technology. If they can't – go get your bag of rocks.

Flash ■ For those that want to be flashy.

Flash is one of the coolest things to hit the web since the Dancing Baby! You've got to remember the Dancing Baby! It was an animated baby dancing to

"Hooked on a Feeling" by Blue Swede (the ugachaka song). It even made a guest appearance on *Ally McBeal*. If you don't remember you can see it on my website www.LarryBailin.com/ugachaka.

Anyway...where was I? Oh yeah...flash. Flash is the animation technology responsible for all those animated movie type intros that you have to wait for, before entering certain websites. If you're like me and most Internet users you hit the "Skip Intro" button while the movie is still loading. Just a little tidbit of information for those taking notes: the "Skip Intro" button is typically clicked on in about a tenth of a second. Makes you wonder why people are even developing these flash movies. Not for the user. In the end, it usually ends up being for themselves. Did I mention all this before? I think I did but it's my personal quest to rid the business world of flash intros!

Most people think they have a great website because it's flashy and creative. The fact is that most visitors skip right by the flash intro to get to the meat and potatoes of the website. A flashy, animated, overdone approach does not a great website make. Creativity for the sake of creativity is just as bad as technology for the sake of technology. If you overuse technology and creativity on your website, you might actually be able to feel the money being sucked out of your coffers.

I've even seen entire websites created using flash technology. The navigation is animated, content is an unspiderable image trapped inside a tiny little frame, and you have to use unnatural up and down arrows to scroll. These types of sites typically have enough music and sound effects to become an opening act on the Vegas Strip.

I have no problem admitting that flash is very cool, and it takes a lot of creative talent and skill (and money) to create flash intros and websites. Still, the fact remains that flash is an animation technology. Animation is slow loading. Remember that only 50% of America has high-speed internet access. Animation is image heavy and music is not the greatest thing to incorporate into a website. I mentioned earlier that over 60% of Internet users surf the web from work – and music is a visitor killer.

Furthermore, *Flash* is not a search engine friendly technology. Although search engines have made great strides over the years to try and index flash sites, they are just not there yet. All things being equal, if your site is developed in flash, or has a flash intro, and your competitor's site does not, they win.

There are good uses of flash technology. I've seen some great "on-demand" product tours and service demos created using flash. The company that does some of the video taping of my presentations uses flash to play on-demand videos on their website (www.eVideoProductions.net). The reason they use flash is that it is more compatible with today's web browsers than other forms of software used to view video. That is a great use of flash.

You can even incorporate flash components into a website to make it a little…well…flashier, without compromising usability and search engine placement. Feel free to add some flash here or there, but don't get carried away. Again, just as technology for the sake of technology helps no one, flash for the sake of flashiness helps no one, either. A talented and creative flash programmer can think of good ways to increase persuasive momentum, without slowing your site down.

Content Management ■ A good manager knows when not to manage.

Content management is a fantastic tool that allows for the (you guessed it) management of your website content. Content management tools allow you to change the content and imagery on your website without having to know HTML programming. HTML stands for Hyper Text Markup Language, and is the programming language used for website development. Essentially, one can access this tool by logging on to a secure area of their website, using any computer with Internet access. You can then edit any page of the website with the ease of filling out a form and hitting the submit button.

I'm a big proponent of content management. Content management tools make it easy for you to update information on your website, which keeps the content fresh and relevant. I'm all for anything that maintains the relevancy of a website. Search engines also tend to give preferential placement to frequently updated sites.

There are some, but not many, pitfalls to using content management tools. Content management tools utilize a database to house content for the website. These databases make your content "dynamic", meaning the content on each page does not exist until someone requests it. Once requested, content, page layout, and imagery are pulled together on the fly. The reason is that content managers don't actually access your website, but are instead communicating with, and updating, content located in the database.

The opposite of dynamic content is "static" content. Static content exists directly on the pages of your website, and employs no database. You would need to use an HTML editing tool such as Adobe Dreamweaver® or Microsoft Front Page® to edit your website. These tools utilize WYSIWYG interfaces (pronounced wizzywig), which stands for "what you see is what you get." These WYSIWYG tools work much like a word processing program. While they typically do not require knowledge of HTML, it is helpful to at least understand the basics when using this type of application.

You really need to think about the pages on your site that could benefit from a content management system. You might not need to change too many of the pages of your website on a regular basis. If you're not making changes more than once a month, you're probably better off with a static website. The less technology used, the better off you'll be.

If you are going to use a content management tool, please be certain that it is search engine friendly. There are many that are, but more that are not. Ask your developer to ensure they are using one that is. I'd even ask to see websites they have developed using whatever content management tools they are going to be using on your site. Check to see if these websites show up in the major search engines (Google, MSN, Yahoo! Ask, Lycos, etc.). Do some comprehensive searches for these sites, and the categories under which they fall. Now be fair; they may not have done any search engine optimization (shame on them), so be very specific with the phrases you use. Include the city and state for the company, in combination with the products or services they offer. Be as specific as possible. You just want to make sure the site can be indexed.

That's about all there is to content management. Great tools, as long as they are not overused and remain search engine friendly.

Search Engine Optimization ■ Buyer Beware!

Now in an attempt to be fair, I'm going to pick apart my own industry, which is search engine optimization, or search engine marketing (SEO or SEM). No one in the industry can seem to agree on what to call it. I like to use SEO, and it's my book. SEO it is.

Just as website programmers have few standard ways of doing things, SEO and SEM have even less. SEO was once viewed as a kind of "black art", just like voodoo and psychic readings. (Is an obese psychic still called a medium? Just wondering.) You could never tell what the optimizer was doing, and whether or not it worked. All you knew was that more traffic seemed to be coming to your site from somewhere, and you wrote a check to someone for something.

Again, shame on you for not insisting on knowing exactly what is being done to your website. When it comes to SEO, you need to *completely* understand what the optimizer is doing. You absolutely must understand what is being done to your website to ensure achievement of the desired results. You have no idea how easy it is to do something, in the name of SEO, that will completely wreak havoc on your website. I have never seen a shadier group of individuals than those calling themselves SEO firms, or so-called SEO experts. Now, that having been said, there are some truly great firms doing things properly. For instance, my company, Single Throw, can help you achieve fantastic results. I'm well aware of the shameless plug I just administered, but it's my book dammit! Still, be careful. For every good provider, there are 50 bad ones.

Before I teach you what to look out for, I'm going to first tell you why it's important to be careful. Like any other skill, SEO requires talent and a broad understanding of marketing, customer behavior, website design and usability, business and sales processes, and technology. Unless a SEO provider can prove quantifiable knowledge in all these areas, they simply shouldn't be working for you.

SEO done in a half-assed or inexperienced manner will do more harm than good. Did you know that you can actually get banned from a search engine? (Trick question. I mentioned it earlier.) It's true. If Google determines that your website is employing technology or tactics designed to trick their algorithms into better placement, you can be black listed from their search engines. Considering that more than 70% of American Internet users find their desired products and services through search engines, it sure would stink to get banned.

Search engines frown upon those trying to trick them. Tricking a search engine using technology or unscrupulous tactics is called "search engine spamming." Hereafter, we'll refer to it as SES, so I don't have to type as much. Then, I can get this book done so you can read it.

This point is relevant enough to risk a little redundancy. SES is done in many ways. One such way is by using software to "cloak" a website. Cloaking employs technology that determines whether an actual person or search engine spider is visiting your website. When a person visits the site they see an "unoptimized" website. When a spider comes to the site they see a heavily optimized piece of crap. This is typically a multitude of pages which stuff an obscene amount into the site that would overwhelm anyone who saw it. In fact, remember that scene in *Raiders of the Lost Ark* where the Germans' faces melt after they open the ark? It would be like that...but with more screaming.

The long and short of it is that cloaking is a bad technique that will get you banned. Rule of thumb – any method requiring the creation of anything an actual visitor cannot see is spam. This includes cloaking, redirects, doorway pages, etc. If it is not intended for visitors, then it was only created to gain placement. Don't do it.

You'll only want to employ techniques that you are comfortable showing to a visitor. To clarify a bit more, it is perfectly fine to create pages outside of your website that are category, topic or even product-specific, as long as those pages are intended to help actual visitors. These topic-specific websites have to provide great information on the relevant topic, while remaining well-designed and functional. It should always follow the same formatting and content-specific rules of your main site.

There are many reasons to use topic-specific pages. Let's say that you're using a slightly older shopping engine that is not search engine friendly, but contains most of your product information. Rather than scrapping an expensive shopping engine, you might simply want to make some product-specific pages to draw attention toward your offerings. The visitor can then click through to your main website to get more information or make a purchase. These pages can be created to serve many purposes and they remain an excellent way to extend the reach of your website.

Putting invisible text on a website is another trick used by spammers. White text on a white background is one example, it remains invisible to the visitor but is still quite viewable for the spider. This is often referred to as "the oldest trick in the book" (at least the oldest trick in this book). Remember, spam is any information not viewable by the visitor.

I've seen tons of websites where the text is specifically placed below the fold, in order to get read by the search engine. This is not something that will get you banned, but it is what I would categorize as a poor attempt by a less than talented SEO professional (used loosely), or "hack." I even see this technique used on the websites of actual SEOs. There is a good sign for you – if you see this technique incorporated into the site of your prospective SEO firm – look them squarely in the eye and laugh hysterically. Then stop abruptly and whisper the word "loser."

Think about this method of stuffing content onto the bottom of a page. It's typically a very small font and often times is a grammatical mess. What if a potential client actually read it? They'd think you were an idiot. Only put content on your website worth reading. Be proud of your content and put it where it can and will be read – at the top of the page.

The long and short of it is that there are no shortcuts to doing SEO right. A great SEO company will not only guide you into a strong search engine showing, but will ensure you maintain a functional, well-designed website that you'll be proud to show your customers. You'll have a website that is geared for success. Great SEO companies do not use tricks, software, cloaking or any other questionable tactics. Common sense, coupled with true marketing, sales, and business acumen are the telltale signs of great SEO.

Bad SEO consultants walk among us and go unnoticed to the untrained eye. They look and act just like us. They have adopted our ways and fit into our culture. You could be sitting next to one right now and not even know it. In John Carpenter's movie, "They Live" (which starred legendary professional wrestler, Rowdy Roddy Piper), aliens took on human form and infiltrated earth's society. You could only tell someone was an alien by wearing a special pair of sunglasses. I am going to help you to identify the bad SEOs. Together, we will foil their plan to bring down the Internet by getting site after site banned from the search engines. Perhaps it's not that dramatic, but it could save you a little heartache and a lot of money. And, come on, what other business book have you read that mentioned Rowdy Roddy Piper?

Red flag means stop

Here is a list of things that I would personally consider "Red Flags." These would either stop me from choosing a specific SEO company or at least induce me to dig further.

Red Flag #1 ▪ The shoemaker's kid's excuse.

Anyone selling you anything should be a believer in their product or service. Knowing that a strong search engine position can generate great qualified leads, a skilled SEO professional should

The shoemaker's kid's excuse refers to the tale surrounding the children of the shoemaker, who remain barefoot because their father is too busy making shoes for others.

have an optimized website of his or her own. Ask them to show you the results for five key phrases, which are relevant to their business. At the very least, they should be using their own service. Ask to see their web stats. This will show the search terms people are using to find their site. If they give you the shoemaker's kid's excuse, tell them it's unacceptable. If the service they offered was any good, they would be using it themselves. They should show up under specific target phrases in at least some of the major search engines.

How friendly is their website? Does it maintain the strong standards mentioned throughout this book? Does it have well-written, professional content that speaks to your needs? Is it professional and easy to navigate? Do they incorporate all those best practices you want for your site?

Red Flag #2 ▪ The bullet point specialist.

Internet marketing should not be a bullet point lost in a sea of unrelated offerings on a website. Internet marketing is a specialty and requires a genuine professional. You need to be wary of web development companies, ad agencies, or other marketing and technology companies that seem to provide Internet marketing and SEO services as a secondary offering.

Nowadays, it seems as though virtually every web development entity lists SEO or Internet as a service. While I understand their desire to perform these services, I have little faith in the performance capabilities of these types of companies.

Red Flag #3 ▪ Keywords.

I mentioned in an earlier chapter that META keywords are no longer used by search engines to determine relevancy, so I'm not going to harp on this issue. Just remember that if a company's strategy toward search engine success is built around the insertion of website keywords, they have no idea what they are doing.

Red Flag #4 ▪ The wacky claims.

I've dedicated a whole chapter to the "guarantee," so I don't want to beat a dead horse. Still, just for the sake of getting an important point across, any company that offers "guaranteed" organic search engine placement is full of crap. No one can guarantee anything in a search engine except the search engines themselves – and they won't. That's all I have to say about the guarantee. Let's talk about the wacky claims.

I've seen some pretty strange claims on SEO websites, but some of the craziest have been in email. I get spam email every day from SEO companies that "guarantee" my placement at the top of search engines. Some of them claim to have special relationships with the search engines, which empowers them to achieve their preferable rankings. No one – but *no one* – has a "special relationship" with a search engine. Search engines do not partner, consult, or give preferential treatment to any company, without exception. This is pure BS.

On another note, you really need to ask yourself whether it's a good idea to do business with a company marketing their services through spam. If they are using unscrupulous methods to market to you, how reputable can they be? Do you really want to trust your image, good name and potential customers to these people?

Another red flag is the promise of submission to a ridiculous number of search engines. As I've mentioned, there are only a dozen or so major search engines, which account for roughly 98% of all domestic searches. I've read claims from companies offering inclusion in tens of thousands of search engines. Simply put: don't fall for it. Big red flag.

You'd be better off setting your money on fire. At least it will keep you warm.

Red flag # 5 ■ The disclaimer.

You almost always see the disclaimer after you see the guarantee. Disclaimers are usually put in place to cover the ass of an overzealous SEO firm, and are typically just the fine print for irresponsible claims. The wackiest disclaimer I've ever seen was on the website for one of those companies advertising Internet marketing as an additional service. I'm going to para-phrase, to avoid distorting any copyright.

This one was actually titled "Liability Disclaimer," which seems a pretty ridiculous thing to have on any website. A liability disclaimer belongs on a contract, and not in the fine print of a page designed to inspire customer contact.

They started off by not guaranteeing first page results when search engine optimization is the only existing method of website marketing, so far so good. Then it got murky. They went on to state that search engines incorporate a keyword/banner buying system, and highest placement could only be ensured by purchasing the right keywords and banners. Huh? The next part was equally puzzling. They indicated that search engines perform an analysis of your keywords, and measure them against your type of business, which creates the formula for determining your ranking. (Larry scratches his head.) Now, just when I think this disclaimer has achieved all the prop-erties of absurdity, they mention that the banner/keyword buying thingy requires on-going processes performed by the search engine programmers. I'm not sure whether they're talking about their program-mers, or those working for the Google's of the world.

The disclaimer closed by promising their clients search engine placement on the first three pages, within *one week of implementation*, provided they spend an amount "reasonably" in line with their competition. Then, they immediately backed off the one week claim by saying that no set timetable to achieve results truly exists. Yup. Not sure it gets any better than that.

This is a real disclaimer on a real website from a real company offering SEO services. (I guess the term "real company" is open to debate.) **Wow!** That's just about as confusing a group of words as I've ever encountered.

Let's look at this a bit. Search engines do not use keyword or banner ad purchases as part of their organic placement formula. It simply does not matter how much you spend on banner ads or pay per click keywords. These programs do not influence your results in any way, and it's irresponsible to suggest otherwise.

I can't even begin to try and explain what the hell this disclaimer is supposed to be disclaiming. Nor can I figure out what this company is actually going to do for you. My guess is they will take your money and make you cry.

Beware of outrageous claims and even more outrageous disclaimers. If it sounds too good to be true – it is.

Now, every SEO company should provide some sort of statement that properly sets expectations. You should know what to expect from your SEO program. While it should not come in the form of a "disclaimer," there should be something in writing, which details timelines, costs, measurements, maintenance, etc. Not having this is not necessarily the sign of a bad SEO provider. However, it does make it incumbent upon you to make sure that expectations, on both sides, are clear and mutually agreeable.

Red flag # 6 ■ You had me at "hello."

Hello, I was just on your website and thought that it was a really great website and my customers would love to see it. I put a link to your website on my links page and was wondering if you would be so kind as to do the same and link to me? My website address is `www.this-is-a-scam-you-gullible-bastard.com.`

Remember, people that email you out of the blue and start with friendly greetings such as "Hello!" or "Dear fellow business owner" should be examined very carefully. The text above is from an actual email I have received numerous times (the URL is made up). These are people trying to artificially increase links to their website by trying to inflate their "link popularity." They compile a huge list of websites and list them on some random page buried deep within their site. The same email is then sent off to thousands of website owners, in hopes of tricking them into placing a link on their page.

This linking strategy will not work. Beware of this tactic. Make sure there is a good reason to create mutual links. You don't want to link to random businesses. In order for them to inspire better search engine placement, or retain any value to your site, they must be relevant to your operation.

There are plenty of issues associated with my industry, and you'll need to stay on your toes. If you are reading this book, it's likely that you are a forward thinking individual with a good deal of common sense. Use your head to scrutinize those making wild claims and unsubstantiated promises. Be skeptical, be paranoid, be careful...and you'll be fine.

14

MOMMY, ARE WE THERE YET?

Yes DEAR, we've reached the end of the book.

Yes, dear readers, we've reached the end. You've made it through the book, and are now free to write that fantastic Amazon.com review, to which I so subtly alluded at the start of the book.

Since I'm big on setting expectations, I'm going to do a little expectation setting now.

I've read many business, marketing, and sales books, and have yet to find one that didn't provide me with at least one practical solution or enhancement. I'm hoping to have helped you achieve at least this much useful guidance.

From within the information contained on these pages, you should be able to pick at least one item to implement and make an immediate change in your business. If this book has inspired even a small change in your mindset about the Internet, and its potential effects on your business and customers, then it was certainly worth writing.

I wrote this book to make businesses aware of the constant changes to both online and offline marketing methods alike.

Changes in business can be a good thing, if you adapt accordingly. Those not addressing and embracing the constant changes within today's business world can suffer through difficult consequences. My career has been spent helping businesses understand and adapt to the changes being brought about by the Internet. The bits of my approach, which I've included in this book, can certainly help any business.

Try to be open-minded, and take a look at your business from the outside in. See things from your customer's perspective. Done well, it will result in your making a better connection with your customers, and will ultimately grow your business.

You just made a very minor investment that can have a profound return. You spent less than thirty dollars on a book containing the perspective of someone with a proven track record of growing businesses from virtually every industry, and of almost every variety. In relation to the overall financial investment you've likely made to market your business and sell your wares, the cost of this book is just a small expenditure. I hope this proves to make it even more valuable. Once you've taken away your personal lessons from this book, pass it along to a co-worker or colleague so they can begin learning as well. By the time the book is done circulating throughout your company, everyone will have taken at least their one thing away, and you'll have created a better informed company with a broad tapestry of understanding. (By the way, there's no law against buying a few copies of the book, and handing them out as gifts. Just making that clear.)

So there it is – I've set my expectations. You should be able to take at least one thing you've learned and integrate it into your marketing arsenal, and make back at least double your investment in the price of this book. Now of course I say this in jest. I am sure you will make back *way more* than sixty bucks. If you can't then this might not have been the right book choice for you. How about something from the *Dick and Jane* collection?

A little focus, a little determination, and you're in. Still, if it doesn't work out…no yelling…I hate that.

All kidding aside, I hope you did benefit from at least some of the material and ideas found within this book. It was my desire to share some of the information and knowledge I've accumulated over the years. If I've helped encourage a difference in your understanding, and given you a chance to grow your business, then it was well worth the effort.

Thanks for letting me into your lives, your heads and your businesses. Visit the official website for the book: MommyWhereDoCustomersComeFrom.com for articles, news, Upcoming speaking engagements etc.

To read my blog visit: ConnectedCustomers.net. To listen to my Podcast visit MomentsInMarketing.com. Feel free to shoot me an email from time to time if you have a question or are looking for a worthy person to include in your will.

Mommy, does everyone now know where customers come from?

Yes Dear.

...and they marketed happily ever after.